'A book this gimmicky has no right to be so funny.'
Ed Grenby, *Radio Times*

'The whole household just love this fun and well-written book. How Ted managed to do it is simply amazing, we all knew he had talent and this book is testament to that. Seriously though, this book is really good and just as silly as you'd expect.' **Saffron**

'I was really sad to finish the book. I would love to meet Ted in person!' **Mark**

'It is a true tail wagger not a shaggy dog story. Witty tail of the true star of *Gone Fishing*.' **Iain**

'I bought this as a gift for my husband who is a fan of the series. He thoroughly enjoyed the book and often read funny snippets out to us.' **Caroline**

'I have thoroughly enjoyed reading *Ted*. So funny, it made me laugh a lot. A real joy. I'm hoping for a follow up soon, please. Would definitely recommend. Here's hoping for a speedy return of his briefcase. LOL.' **Katy**

'I found myself chuckling at the witty insights into Ted's personality and his interactions with the humans around him, with his gruff voice echoing in my mind as I delved into the pages. It's a delightful escape into the world of fishing camaraderie and banter that fans have come to love. Each page is infused with humour and warmth. If you share my passion for Paul and Bob's adventures, this book will undoubtedly bring a smile to your face and warmth to your heart.' **Vijay**

'We absolutely loved this book – it gave us many a laugh, plus, a lovely insight into a dog's life – and Bob's mind!!' **Janet**

'This book could quite possibly be the best book I've ever read! If you love the programme *Gone Fishing* with Paul & Bob, you will absolutely love it.' **Mel**

'When you are feeling dog-eared, dog-tired or dog-beat, read *Ted the Dog*. It's the best pick-me-up ever!' **Leonard**

'I picked the book up to read a few pages and didn't put it down until I had read it from cover to cover. I laughed so much my sides and chest hurt, tears of laughter streaming down my face.' **Burt**

'A fabulous book, loved it and some very important messages in there too. If you are a dog lover, you will love this book.' **Julie**

A Pawtobiography

TED

A Pawtobiography

My adventures on *Gone Fishing*

TED THE DOG

(As told to Lisa Clark)

EBURY
SPOTLIGHT

EBURY SPOTLIGHT

UK | USA | Canada | Ireland | Australia
India | New Zealand | South Africa

Ebury Spotlight is part of the Penguin Random House group of companies
whose addresses can be found at global.penguinrandomhouse.com

Penguin Random House UK
One Embassy Gardens, 8 Viaduct Gardens, London SW11 7BW

penguin.co.uk
global.penguinrandomhouse.com

First published by Ebury Spotlight in 2024

This paperback edition published in 2025

2

Typeset by seagulls.net

Printed and bound in Great Britain by Clays Ltd, Elcograf S.p.A.

The authorised representative in the EEA is Penguin Random House Ireland,
Morrison Chambers, 32 Nassau Street, Dublin D02 YH68.

A CIP catalogue record for this book is available from the British Library

ISBN 9781529965896

*For Dolly. You loved me your whole life,
I will miss you for the rest of mine.*

CONTENTS

Foreword

Ted was born in 2012. He was given as a surprise Christmas present and then dumped in the New Year when he was only six months old. He went into a foster home to be assessed and was then handed to a rescue centre, before being adopted into his forever home in 2013, where he still lounges to this day, unless he is fishing with Paul and Bob, of course.

PART ONE

CHAPTER 1

Every Dog Has Its Day

Right, listen up. This is how it all unfolded for me. This is the story of how I went from homeless and boneless to famous and fearless. Nearly every word of this is true. You can work out for yourselves which bits are exaggerated, or not. It's up to you, I'm not bothered either way.

My early motivation to stand out from the crowd came from two very different chaps:

Daniel Craig – he was homeless, sleeping on park benches, before finding fame as an actor and becoming one of our favourite Bond stars.

Harry Houdini – he ran away from home aged twelve and worked on the streets before he became arguably the world's greatest escape artist.

I can relate to both of them. I too turned initial misfortune into great success.

I also like to think I have the charisma of Craig and I know I have the skills of Houdini.

Sitting on a Welsh riverbank basking in the sun, watching those two muppets Mortimer and Whitehouse fishing together on the River Wye, I looked back at how I'd managed to land so firmly on my grubby little paws.

With the sound of birdsong, the gentle lapping of the water and their laughter reverberating around the valley, there was nowhere else I'd rather be.

Apart from maybe supervising a controlled explosion or taking a trip to the Museum of Naval Firepower, which is in Gosport if you ever fancy joining me.

It wasn't always like this.

I was a skinny, unwanted runt.

Now I am a slightly portly B-list canine celebrity – and I wouldn't change a thing about how I got here. It's been quite the rollercoaster but instead of howling, I chose to strap in and enjoy the ride.

Everything you are about to read is highly classified and once you have finished this book you must destroy it immediately – either eat it or bury it, the choice is yours.

Why am I writing this book?

I need my voice to be heard. Don't get me wrong, I love my co-stars Messrs Mortimer and Whitehouse but they don't always know what really goes on inside my head. Mind you, nor do I most of the time.

I also need to speak up for all the other dogs out there, the ones who are abandoned or misunderstood or mistreated. I want to do this for them, I need to give them a voice and I am in the privileged position of being able to do just that.

I'm proud to say I am now an integral part of *Gone Fishing*, even though I have never laid my paws on a rod or sniffed a fish.

I mostly wander around the riverbanks, eavesdropping on Paul and Bob's conversations, nicking their food and trying not to tread on their fishing rods. I excel at the food part, not so much minding the rods. Why do they leave them where such an athletic dog like me can so easily trip over them? If I've heard Paul say 'mind the rod' once, I've heard it a million times. Well, I would have if I ever listened to him, which I don't.

I am in the unique position of being able to tell you what goes on behind the scenes from the ankles up when the cameras are not rolling and what working with Bob and Paul is really like.

But first, I need to tell you how life started out for me, which from the outset was not looking too rosy, to say the least.

CHAPTER 2

A Star is Born

I was born in the summer of 2012, one of six puppies. Three girls, three boys.

They immediately put nail varnish on our toes to distinguish us from each other, which was not quite the welcome I had expected, and the acrid smell lingered for days.

I was the last born and seemingly took everyone by surprise when I popped out as no one was expecting me. I guess that might have been an early omen.

I think I'm a Patterdale terrier. Or mostly a Patterdale terrier. I sent off for a DNA test, which had quite surprising results, but more of that later … plot twist, I apparently contain traces of Malinois.

I've read that Patterdales are a working breed and were bred exclusively to hunt foxes and vermin. It didn't say they would make a good fishing companion, so we can ignore all the experts for a start, but I am a hard worker.

The origins of Patterdales can be traced way back to the early twentieth century and a breeder called Joe Bowman. Big up Joe. He certainly knew a top dog when he saw one.

The funniest thing I read about Patterdales was that their stubbornness, energy and hunting instincts can make them difficult to train.

Difficult to train? I was impossible. When will you humans learn to read the small print?

Anyway, I came out fighting, eyes firmly shut and mouth wide open, ready for whatever this world was going to lob my way.

My mother was aloof at best and I never met my father. I think it was just a one-night stand and Mum never spoke of him again. I always imagined him to be an incredibly handsome, strong dog with loose morals but a good heart.

As I was the last puppy to be born, my siblings would tease me, calling me a little shrimp. I was certainly the smallest, but I had enough teeth for all of them. Even before I was able to open my eyes, I used my tongue to lick my face and thought I had something stuck in my mouth, only to realise they were teeth. And they were sharp little teeth.

Right from the start I knew I was different from my brothers and sisters, not just because of my looks but because of my attitude. They whinged and whined and cried and huddled together but I felt independent, I felt different. I didn't need any security from them and nestled alone in my own corner.

I knew I was born to be a fighter and a survivor.

I was determined to make my dad proud, even if he may never witness it for himself.

When dogs are left on their own, they go into what is known as survival mode, when their natural instincts kick in. They have an increased alertness and become hypervigilant.

It takes different dogs a different amount of time to reach this state. For some it can take weeks, for others it may be days. I was literally born with it.

You've heard of fight or flight? I had fight *and* flight. Bare my teeth and nick off.

I was born with the normal number of teeth for a puppy – 28. But what made me stand out from the pack was the size of my bottom teeth, which were always rather eye catching. And tongue catching as it turned out. I had to learn to live with the protrusion and I quickly mastered how to harness the power of those teeth.

They did drop out as I grew up, but those 28 were replaced with a further 42. Twenty on the top and 22 big ones proudly standing to attention at the bottom. I remember the day I first looked in a mirror. I stood and stared at myself for a good ten minutes. I tried to curl my bottom lip over my bottom teeth but it wouldn't stretch that far, so I decided to simply grin and bear it.

The official term for my artistic dentistry is an 'underbite'. I call it my superpower.

The home I was born into smelt quite rank, there was a real stale doggy whiff about the place. I sniffed my own paw pits, but I don't think it was all down to me. The room we were all in was small and cramped and frankly there were just too many of us sharing a space.

There was barely any room to swing a cat, which is a shame as that would have been a really fun way to pass the time in those early days of life.

CHAPTER 3

Puppy Love

It was dull being a puppy. I had to hang around the house all day, I wasn't allowed to go out and I was only fed grit. Well, it tasted like grit, it was dry and flavourless, although it turns out this was good training for my later culinary adventures on the riverbanks with Bob.

The other pups lapped up their food, which just proved my initial theory about them – they had no taste.

Even simple things in those early days were a pain in the butt. Literally.

I mean, a man's gotta do what a man's gotta do but every time I needed to do my business I was unceremoniously grabbed from behind and lobbed outside, even when it was pouring with rain and with no suitable reading material either. If I was left alone, I might have gone quicker. It's not easy to answer the call of nature when you are being closely monitored.

The fuss made when I did what I was put outside to do was ridiculous. 'Yay! Well done, what a clever boy,' they'd say as they applauded me. I'm surprised they didn't order a bloody brass band and get out the bunting.

Those early days dragged and the nights seemed endless. My siblings carried on crying and moaning, especially when I crept up behind them in the pitch dark and nipped their tails with my teeth. They didn't really like me very much and I know they talked about me behind my back. I often heard them calling me a right runt.

They didn't let me join in with any of their games either, which actually I was thankful for. I didn't want to play chase, particularly in a room that was about the size of a garden shed. It might actually have been a garden shed, come to think about it.

The TV was on in the house 24/7. I was fascinated by the way humans can just sit and stare at a big screen for hours on end without moving a muscle. It was like they had slipped into a coma as soon as that box was brought to life.

Most of what was on seemed like a load of crap to me.

Britain's Got Talent – they absolutely didn't.

I'm A Celebrity Get Me Out of Here – why the hell go there in the first place?

I thought Ant and Dec were the only people permitted to present a television show in the UK, they were never off the screens.

Remember, this was in the days before *Gone Fishing* became the best thing on the box.

That particular summer it was also the London Olympics and the football championships, both of which seem to go on endlessly.

I didn't understand why humans always want to compete with each other and push themselves to their upper limits. What's wrong with a pleasant stroll round a field and then spending the rest of the day asleep?

Some sports in the Olympics amused me. I particularly enjoyed the wrestling and the boxing and picked up some useful moves watching those. I would practise throws and takedowns on the other puppies and my left hook would have them all running for cover.

The football was more fun. I was fascinated to watch grown men kick each other instead of the ball, theatrically hurl themselves to the floor when they hadn't even been touched and then weep buckets when they lost the game.

England were beaten in the tournament, losing 4–2 on penalties to Italy, and I quickly gathered that was not particularly good news.

It didn't seem much fun for the humans to watch. They ranted and raved and swore and got themselves into a right two and eight. I learnt some very fruity and very useful new words during Euro 2012.

I did wonder about pursuing a career as a football mascot. But I didn't fancy dressing up in ridiculous outfits. At least I didn't back then. Of course I grew to love it.

CHAPTER 4

Home Alone

The other five puppies left home after about three months. I was glad to see their sorry butts leave the premises and thought me and Mum would have a lovely quiet life together but she made it pretty clear she didn't want me hanging around either. She was always growling at me and telling me off for getting under her paws.

Even though I was offered for sale at half the price of the others, there were no takers.

You might be starting to feel sorry for me and you can pack that in straight away. I'm as tough as I look and I don't need any pity. It was just a difficult time for me and I don't want to dwell any further on it if you don't mind.

Anyway, Christmas was coming and there was so much food around, which I helped myself to (no, not raisins or chocolate, every smart dog knows they could be fatal), I'm talking about cheese and good grief there was tonnes of the stuff. Whenever they left the fridge door open I'd stealthily nip in and lick the nearest portion, being extra careful not to leave any teeth marks. My favourite was Brie

– it was so soft but I think it made my breath smell pretty rank. Not that that would bother anyone, they all kept their distance from me anyway.

That Christmas, everyone in the house seemed in a really good mood, particularly in the evenings, although they were extra grumpy in the mornings. They were drinking gallons of something. I don't know if it was some kind of competition or a group sport but night after night they tried to empty more bottles. Every morning I was woken by the horrendous noise of glass bottles being lobbed into the recycling. It gave me a terrible headache and was not a good start to the day. Why couldn't they just all share a bowl to drink from and why were they all so bloody thirsty anyway?

I was growing up and becoming more adventurous by the day. Mum said I was becoming more of a pain in the arse every day so I tried to keep out of her way.

I learnt to climb the Christmas tree at night, using my teeth as crampons. I would time myself to get to the very top and touch the hideous fairy, with penalty points for any baubles that smashed to the floor. My PB was 30 seconds, with three smashed baubles, which I would simply sweep to the back of the tree so I didn't get found out.

I was nearly caught when the family noticed how bare the tree was looking because of all the pine needles I had dislodged but all they did was complain about the quality of the tree and the price they'd paid for it. I think the whole thing is pointless anyway. Why chop a healthy tree down and let it die slowly inside the house and then lob it out after a month or so?

I was looking forward to Christmas Day as I was convinced I would get a new toy, given I was the only one left, but instead on Christmas Eve a man and a woman came round and examined me from head to paw. They called me 'cute', which made me want to throw up, and they laughed at my teeth, which made me want to throw up some more on their shiny shoes.

After they handled me like a sack of spuds, a deal was done and in exchange for a crate of beer and a family pack of iced mince pies, they took me away in their car. I barked goodbye to Mum but she simply rolled over, grunted and went back to sleep.

It was an odd feeling, leaving the only place I knew without a clue as to where I was headed next.

I had all my worldly goods, which was a threadbare blanket and a tiny mirror, neatly packed into my leather briefcase in the back of the car.

You know how music often triggers memories? As we started our journey there was a song playing on the radio, which kind of became my song. It was 'Don't You Worry Child' by Swedish House Mafia. I decided not to worry and to accept whatever fate was going to throw at me.

CHAPTER 5

Home 2.0

The new house smelt better than the last one but on my first night there I was kept in a tiny, dark room and wasn't allowed to see anyone. I wondered if it was a kind of quarantine. It was a long night but I managed to perfect a forward roll, which I thought was a pretty neat trick. I did keep banging into the walls and getting a bit dizzy but it kept me amused.

The next morning a horrible scratchy red bow was placed on my head and I was put in a cardboard box. I was furious. Was this some kind of sick game? I'd seen this happen on *SAS: Are You Tough Enough?* so I wasn't scared but I did wonder what they were going to interrogate me about. Was it my tree climbing? I really hoped it wasn't anything to do with my briefcase.

I was carried out of the room, squashed tightly in the box, and was presented to two lively boys, who I'd say were about 10 and 12 years old. I thought this was promising. I was sure they'd like to wrestle and fight and I was bang up for that. But then one of them picked me up and burst into tears, which was somewhat disappointing and a little over the top, I thought. Maybe my teeth upset him? Apparently not, as I heard them talking about tears of happiness, whatever the heck those are. Are humans the only ones who have two kind of tears? I have actually only cried once in my life – as you'll find out later if you stick with this story. If you don't, I'm not bothered, it's of no concern to me either way.

Both boys smelt pretty bad. A heady mix of paraffin and pizza. I know I've banged on quite a bit about smells but do you realise a dog has 300 million smell receptors in their nose? Humans have a somewhat pathetic 6 million. Let that sink in and perhaps think more carefully before you break wind in front of a dog's nose. And while we're on the subject, stop blaming the dog. You know who you are.

I heard the boys say they'd always wanted a puppy so I did think my luck had changed for the better. For all of about one hour, I was the best thing that had ever happened to them.

They chased me around the living room and we played a great game of hide and seek. Then they wandered back to their gaming consoles and pretty much forgot all about me. I spent over an hour hiding beneath the sofa before I realised they'd stopped looking for me.

They called me Billy. It was a name that didn't suit me. I always thought I was more of a Ronnie or a Reggie. I didn't come to them when they called me, in protest at the name.

They said my 'recall' was terrible, but their engagement with me was nothing to shout about either, so what did they expect?

I will admit to being pretty destructive around the house. It was something to do and it got their attention when I gnawed at a table leg or ate the skirting board. I wanted to keep my teeth in good nick. I always knew they were a gift and I used to sharpen them outside on rocks and stones whenever I got the chance.

I loved it when it rained. I would stand for hours over a puddle, checking my reflection in the water and perfecting my toothy grin. I also liked trotting back into the house and leaving footprints all over the kitchen floor. I got yelled at for doing that but what was I supposed to do, wear shoes and socks when I went outside and change into my slippers when I got in?

If they did shout at me for leaving paw prints, I'd go and wipe my feet on the nearest rug and finish with a long, satisfying bum scoot for good measure.

I quickly learnt how to amuse myself in those early days.

Let me make one thing clear before we continue: I wasn't naughty, I was just as bored of them as they were

of me. They clearly hadn't seen that famous sticker: 'A dog is for life, not just for Christmas.' They obviously thought a dog was for about an hour, two at a stretch.

CHAPTER 6

Into the Woods

Walks with the family were pretty rare so I used to take myself out and spend hours in the woods alone. I don't think they ever noticed I'd gone.

I'd make myself a little packed lunch from anything I could grab from the fridge, usually leftovers or, if I was lucky, cocktail sausages and cheese, which I'd carefully pack into my briefcase. For pudding I'd eat the blackberries that grew all around the forest. They made my teeth turn purple but that was like camouflage and just made me look and feel more like a warrior.

I was a big fan of *Our Girl*, I could really relate to Molly who joined the army when her life was going down the drain. I don't think the forces would accept a good-for-nothing Patterdale in their ranks, sadly. Anyway, I learnt a lot from watching those military shows.

I taught myself the essential survival skills, like how to start a fire and build underground camps, as well as finding crucial water sources. I discovered that discarded crisp

packets collect rainwater, making them easy to drink from, like a little portable bowl.

I was astounded at the amount of litter in the woods. At first I thought people would come back to pick it up on their way home, but clearly not. Animals.

I lost count of the amount of times I got chewing gum stuck in between my paws. It was impossible to get rid of. I tried to pick it out with my teeth but then it just got stuck there instead. It did make my mouth a little more minty fresh, to be fair, but it really wasn't worth the effort.

I discovered another strange phenomenon deep in the woods, which really freaked me out. And not a lot scares me, as you know by now.

There were all sorts of small, coloured bags tied to the trees and pushed into bushes. The more I looked, the more I saw.

I wondered if it was some satanic ritual or if people had put them there to help them find their way back home. Perhaps it was some form of elaborate tree decoration. It didn't make any sense.

I decided to do some intelligence gathering. I carefully pushed myself into a bush and extracted one of the bags with my teeth, which turned out not to be such a smart idea – one I instantly regretted.

You will not believe what was inside the bag. Dog dirt. They were hanging bags of dog dirt. And they were all over the woods. All sorts of different shapes, sizes and indeed weights.

Did people put them there as some kind of sick trophy?

Can you imagine if us dogs put your excrement into a bag for life and hung it on your fence, or even better, your car wing mirror for all to see? You wouldn't like it, would you, so please don't humiliate your canine friends like that ever again. See it. Say it. Sort your sh*t out.

I would hide out in the camp I carefully built in the woods and put the local squirrels under close surveillance.

I couldn't be bothered to chase them – I knew I'd never catch them because they'd cheat and climb up the nearest tree – so I gave each one a name and a number, which I carefully wrote on a chart.

For example:

No 12. Bobby Fitness

No 22. Daddy Ketchup

No 36. Ron Blaster

No 4. Jen Toogood

No 5. I think was her sister (or a close relative)
    Penny Toogood

No 6. Sandy Peanuts

No 18. Campbell Cloudwater

I kept the chart locked securely in my briefcase, which had a smart combination lock, then I would hide it in the woods every night when I'd finished work for the day before I ambled back to the house, muddy paws and all.

I would also play squirrel bingo, which would sometimes take weeks, as those bushy-tailed pests do tend to look the same from a distance, but I had both the patience and time to tick them all off – and once I had completed a game, I'd start all over again.

I spent most of my time alone and, aside from them putting down a bowl of dry food every other day, I had no interaction with the family. Well, not that they knew about anyway.

I used to nick their mobile phones at night – those handy teeth of mine had a vicelike grip and I could stealthily carry off their prized possessions into a dark corner without causing much disturbance.

I couldn't believe how much time they spent looking at their phones during the day, just staring and staring for hours at a time, with their gobs wide open and one thumb religiously and rhythmically moving up and down. I had one toy – a stuffed ugly cat which I really liked – but I didn't feel the need to stare at it for hours and hours at a time for entertainment.

During the still and quiet of the night I learnt how to text. I bet you didn't know that the pads on our paws work perfectly on a touchscreen phone as they are conductive. At first I just spent my time searching the web for dog treats and googling luxury briefcases but once I mastered the art of texting, I sent what one might call prank messages to random people in the boys' contacts. I'll be honest here, I caused havoc, but it was a hell of a lot of fun, under the circumstances.

There'd be plenty of commotion and shouting first thing in the morning, presumably as a result of what I'd done and particularly because I had run their precious batteries down. I can see how mobile phones are useful but they didn't half cause a lot of stress as well. And god forbid if a mobile was lost or misplaced, it would send the humans into a complete blind panic. So, yes, of course I would hide them from time to time. Wouldn't you?

If they weren't so obsessed with their phones, they wouldn't have got quite so agitated.

I wasn't a model house guest, I admit, but I did appreciate having a roof over my head, although I had a sinking feeling that wasn't going to last. Perhaps it was my fault? But I was still only a puppy. What did they expect from me? I was toilet trained, could use the television remote controls and had actually got quite good at Candy Crush.

CHAPTER 7

Taking Out the Trash

When the family packed up the Christmas decorations, they decided it was time to get rid of me as well. I thought they were going to leave me out with the dead tree on the side of the road but they left me outside an animal rescue centre, which was so thoughtful of them.

I didn't miss the house or those bratty boys one little bit but I missed the woods and then there was the dreadful realisation that I'd left my leather briefcase behind in my camp. I had no idea where I was and how far away I was from the woods. I suddenly felt really cold and thought I was going to throw up. I ate a big clump of grass to calm my stomach.

Luckily the briefcase was locked, of course, so I knew no one could access the contents, but I hated the thought of the squirrels crawling all over it. It was such a beautiful case. And it was all I really had in the world.

Before anyone noticed I was dumped outside the care home, I chewed my way through my lead (those teeth, so handy) and set off in search of the woods, my woods. My compass was also in my briefcase so I had no idea which direction to go in. I tried to follow my nose but even if I'd known what that meant, it didn't work, as my nose was always pointing forwards and going in the same direction as me.

A kindly squirrel stopped to ask if I needed any help. I was instantly wary, but it turned out he was the smart squirrel from Bob Mortimer's novel *The Satsuma Complex*, as I found out later. As I didn't know the name of the woods I used to hide in, he couldn't help me.

Before we parted, the squirrel told me his name was Carlos and said, cryptically, 'You're going to be OK. Trust me and think around that for a while.' Then he went on his way.

Night fell and I got cold and hungry. My firelighters were also in my briefcase so I couldn't make a fire. I ate the little bits of biscuit I had stuck in my teeth from my last dinner but it wasn't nearly enough. I curled myself up into a little ball and went to sleep. I'm a tough guy, there's no doubt about that and I want you to remember it, but I don't mind admitting I was pretty fed up that night. I had no home, no family or friends and more importantly no briefcase. The future looked somewhat dreary.

In the morning, I wandered down the road, dodging cars and playing my own version of chicken just for the thrill of it, until I came back to the building I recognised

as the place where I was left the day before. My lead was still dangling from the post where I was tied up. So I sat down next to it.

The noise coming from inside was deafening. So many different tones of barking and howling. I could easily make out at least eight different breeds – I always thought if I was booked to go on *Celebrity Mastermind*, my specialist subject would be identifying breeds by barks. It was yet another special gift I had.

The deep growl of the German Shepherd. The high-pitched whinge of the poodle. The haughty cry of the greyhound. The irritating yap of the terrier. Even though I was (mostly) a Patterdale terrier, I barked. I never yapped.

Most of the dogs were cussing and swearing. It was a cacophony of filth coming from inside. It wasn't exactly inviting but I wasn't spoilt for choice as to where else to go. If I'd kept one of the boys' mobile phones, I could have called an Uber – but I'm no thief and anyway, where would I go?

CHAPTER 8

Banged Up

I sat outside and waited for my fate to unfold.

Eventually a lady came out of the front door, took one look at me and burst out laughing.

I nearly ran off again but before I could, she picked me up and smiled at me. I did my best smile back, which only made her laugh again.

She told me I was in a sorry state, which I thought was a little harsh. Granted I hadn't cleaned my teeth in a while and my breath was probably quite fruity but I wasn't quite as manky as she was making out.

Turns out I was a bloody Adonis compared to many of the other inmates.

I was put into a cell with a plump beige pug called Peggy and a matted blond poodle called John. Peggy only had three legs and John was an old fella, I'd say at least 12, with very sad eyes and breath to rival mine.

I told them my name was Reggie.

Peggy had only arrived the day before but John had been there for months, ever since his beloved owner died.

They told me it was a safe space. We had a bed each and were fed every evening.

There was no carpet or television or windows and we were locked in our kennels for most of the time, although we did have one-hour exercise sessions twice a day. I loved this yard time when you could mingle with all the other inmates. The dangerous dogs were kept in their own area away from the rest of us, which was a relief, with the worst of them kept in solitary confinement for their own safety.

It didn't take long before I was Top Dog in the yard. The other mutts knew they could come to me with any worries or fears they had and I kept them all in order. I wouldn't stand for any unnecessary aggression and I laid down a zero tolerance policy for bullying. I was respected, probably for the first time in my life. It felt good.

I turned a blind eye to the odd scrap or playful fight. We all had to let off steam sometimes. Considering there were so many breeds and different ages and backgrounds sharing the same space, we all got on fairly well. There was also a large turnover of clientele, so there were always new friends to make – and to impress.

I would regularly hold court, telling anyone who would listen (and those who didn't) about my adventures in the woods, with a small amount of poetic licence, of course.

Their eyes would widen as I told them how I fought off badgers and bears and gnawed through barbed wire with my teeth and they lapped up every word. I told them my tail got caught in a rabbit trap and I'd had to gnaw it off to escape, leaving just a little stump, which still wagged but didn't whoosh, as I demonstrated.

I affectionately call my stump a nubbin.

I didn't want to tell them I was abandoned, so I said I ran away from home to find a better life.

Back in our own kennels, Peggy, John and I continued to get to know each other better. We had our own ground rules though. John didn't want to talk about how his owner died, which we understood. Peggy didn't want to talk about how she lost her leg, which we respected. We assumed it was a skiing accident. I didn't want to talk about my missing briefcase.

Outside our kennel was a little sheet of information pinned to the door with details about each of us.

They said Peggy and John were good around children but couldn't live with cats.

They said little was known about my previous history and they failed to mention my squirrel hobby or my intimate knowledge of explosives, which I thought was a shame as it would have made me quite the commodity.

I don't know exactly how long I lived with Peggy and John but I do remember it was a happy time. We enjoyed each other's company and when it was lights out we'd all squeeze into one bed, with me and Peggy jostling to get furthest away from John's breath.

CHAPTER 9

Party Time

I had my first and very memorable birthday party at the rescue centre. I'd witnessed a few human birthdays and I always thought they were very sorry affairs involving soggy cake, false bonhomie and weedy candles that really weren't worth the effort of lighting. Presents were exchanged and then, rather like when I was a gift, forgotten about and later given to charity. Or worse, re-gifted.

I'd thought a lot about how I'd celebrate my first birthday. I'd dreamt of a massive exploding cake that could splatter dog meat all over the walls. My ideal present would have been some tooth floss and a travel plug, in case anyone asked, which they didn't.

I was trapped in the kennels with no chance of any gifts so Peggy, John and I hatched a plan to make it a night to remember.

Word spread like wildfire in the yard that something big was about to kick off.

The following evening, we managed to get all the dogs on my floor out of their kennels. Did I mention I can pick locks? Another string to my bow. What a night it was. We went hard, staying up all night, bouncing around on each other's beds and making a right mess of the place. Considering his age, John could still throw a few impressive shapes.

I don't even remember going to bed. I think Peggy helped me find my room and held back my ears as I threw up from too much kibble.

The next morning the kennel assistants thought we'd all caught a virus. There was vomit everywhere and most of the dogs stayed in their beds all day, not being able to face any food. No one was rehomed for a week, until we'd all passed another mandatory health check. Everyone agreed it was totally worth it. It gave me further 'legendary' status – but didn't get me any closer to a new home.

Peggy was eventually taken by a lovely family who already had a pug and a couple of kids, who incidentally looked very much like pugs. John was picked by a delightful older lady who said he could simply sit on her lap for the rest of his days. I'll never forget the totally contented looks on their faces as they were led away.

I was really happy for both of them but wondered when and if my time would come. A steady stream of people passed by my cage each week, most of them laughing and then swiftly moving on. Eventually I just stayed in my bed, facing the wall and plotting my escape. I could easily get out if I really wanted to, but I just wasn't sure where I'd head to.

It's not that I'd given up. I just couldn't be arsed to try to please anyone any more.

I remembered the squirrel telling me all would be well but right now I couldn't see how.

I thought about my briefcase probably rotting somewhere in the forgotten woods. I should have booby-trapped it but my wiring skills were not up to scratch back then.

I mentioned my briefcase to some of the lads in the yard. They had mates on the outside and said they'd put the word out in case anyone had come across any lost baggage on their travels but the trail seemed very cold.

In the weeks I was alone in my little cage waiting to be picked, I made up a song, which I'd sing to myself every night.

Pick me up, take me home
I no longer want to be alone
I can light a fire, I can build a camp
I can even rewire a lamp
My teeth are sharp, they'll give you a laugh
So stop walking past, you total dumbass.

Several weeks passed and I got a new housemate. He had huge ears and eyes as wide as wheels. They must have decided to put the facially compromised into the same enclosure.

I reached out my paw to say hi but he came straight up to my face and licked me on both sides of my cheeks.

'Bonjour. Je suis Pierre. Je suis français. Comment ça va?'

This chap was speaking a language I did not understand and it really threw me.

I looked at his paperwork on the outside of our cage.

'Pierre is a one-year-old French Bulldog who was found abandoned on the Channel Tunnel. He has a passport and is keen on travel.'

I was quite envious of Pierre and his travels and wanted to hear all about where he'd come from but the language barrier was an issue for both of us at the start.

He did, however, have a pack of cards and he taught me how to play vingt-et-un. I will admit we did have a bit of a gamble. I won his bed.

We slowly learnt to communicate with each other using our paws and tongues. Dogs use their tongues in a similar way to how you people use your hands. They are very useful for us to communicate and interact with each other. I'll wager our tongues are a lot cleaner than your grubby hands, most of the time.

One morning Pierre said I must have had terrible nightmares during the night, as I had been gritting my teeth and growling and my legs were twitching all over the shop.

I thought he was actually having some kind of a fit as he tried to physically demonstrate this to me, but I eventually got the gist of what he was saying.

I explained that I had probably been dreaming about my lost briefcase. Using my paw, I drew a sketch of what it looked like in the dirt on our floor.

I thought his eyes were about to pop out of his head (they were halfway there already, to be fair). Later that afternoon, in yard time, he quickly led me to a pitbull called Vinnie.

Vinnie had seen my briefcase. He and some of his lads had been chasing a pack of deer through the woods while escaping from their last home when one of them tripped and fell over it. Vinnie now had it stashed under his bed, frustrated he couldn't open it.

He said he'd return it in exchange for me teaching him how to pick locks so he could escape. Apparently, he'd managed to break out from five different homes already but this one was proving to be more problematic. I said I'd happily oblige. I'd have done almost anything to get my paws on that briefcase again and besides, I wasn't going to refuse Vinnie. What he lacked in brains he made up for in pure brawn.

We agreed to meet the following Saturday, when a new influx of felons would arrive, and I could give him a locksmith tutorial in one of the empty gaffs that were being cleaned for the new arrivals.

I can't believe I got so close to getting my briefcase back – only to be thwarted at the last minute.

CHAPTER 10

Coming Home

A couple of days later I was woken very early – I think it was knocking on midday – by loud voices outside my cage.

'I want that one, I want that one,' they were saying over and over again.

For one awful minute I thought Matt Lucas or David Walliams was about to adopt me. I mean, I like comedy as much as the next dog but I'd take Paul and Bob over those two any day.

But it wasn't Matt or Dave, it was a pretty, kindly looking woman and her young son peering at me through the bars. They made a charitable cash donation and before I knew it, my bags were packed and I was in reception checking out, preparing to make my way to my third home.

Would it be third time lucky? It couldn't really be a lot worse than the first home and the second one was a perfectly good stopgap. It just wasn't really the same after Peggy and John left. Although both of them did write to me from time to time so I knew they were happy and settled.

I bade a fond farewell to Pierre, who was happy to stay for the time being as he'd fallen in love with a beautiful Italian greyhound next door called Lotta and I think they were set to move in with each other when I left.

I wondered if I'd fetched a fair price. I'd heard chatter in the kennels that some pedigree dogs (brand new with tags) go for in excess of £2,000 a pop and they come with certificates and receipts and stuff showing their parents and grandparents and their grandparents, which all sounds a bit unnecessary to me.

Second-hand – or used – I was deemed to be worth £100. I reckon if they'd known about my technical skills or vast military knowledge I could have fetched nearer to £500 but it wasn't to be.

I was quickly hustled into the back of a big black car with tinted windows, which suited me down to the ground. I felt really important and maybe even a little bit special for the first time in my life.

Some of my old kennel mates were having exercise time in the yard and I saw their jaws fall open in awe as I left. I used my paw to put the back window down and gave them a regal wave.

Pierre shouted back, 'Au revoir. La vie est belle.' And then, 'Make the most of your freedom and don't do anything that could lead you back here.' Least I think that's what he said via his manic gestures.

Then I caught sight of Vinnie. He was barking furiously and had his paws up in a kind of 'what the hell' gesture. My blood ran cold. In the thrill and excitement of finally being picked for a new home, I'd forgotten all about our deal.

I could only look back in horror as we sped away, leaving behind my precious briefcase once again.

It was a small comfort that I knew where it was, but how the hell was I going to get it back now?

There was no point beating myself up about it. I'd find a way and at least I knew it was safe and locked, of course.

I had to focus on the present. I was on my way to my new life at last. Would this be my forever home or yet another stopgap? I made myself a set of rules to make sure I wasn't kicked out again:

- no indoor explosives
- no house parties
- no nicking stuff
- no indoor climbing

Waiting for me at my new home was the kindest, most gentle giant of a dog I'd ever seen. She was an Old English Sheepdog, called Dolly. She was five years old. She was tall, elegant and statuesque with a beautifully soft, thick white fur coat and a long tail that gently swayed from side to

side. I'd never seen anything quite like her and I will admit to being a little intimidated at first. I wondered if she was actually royalty.

Dolly had a posh voice and smelt incredibly fragrant. Her toenails were manicured and her hair was long and silky. She was most certainly a pedigree, the first I'd ever met, and I wasn't sure how to address her. M'Lady or Ma'am? Should I bow?

I wondered what on earth she made of me as I stood there looking up at her. I knew I stank pretty bad and I hadn't cleaned my teeth that morning as I was in such a hurry to get out of the kennels, so my breath must have been rancid. Maybe she thought I'd just popped in to clear the house of vermin and would soon be on my way.

She sat down next to me and gave me a little sniff. If she did want to recoil, she hid it well.

She put her huge paw on my back and simply said, 'Welcome home.' Then she asked me what my name was.

Did I have a name? I had been Billy, then I was known as Reggie in the kennels, but that seemed somewhat inappropriate in this home. I thought it might be time for a fresh start so I told her I didn't have a name. The only thing I'd ever really been called was a runt. She did recoil at that.

She told me she had a pedigree name, which was 'Fabranese Cup Cake'. It was quite a mouthful, but she

said I could call her Dolly. Just as well as there's no way I could get my sizeable teeth around Fanranese biscuit or whatever it was.

It did make me wonder, if I'd been born in different circumstances, what my kennel name might have been. Perhaps Explosive Billy Big Boy. Yes, I liked that.

Dolly told me she'd lived here her whole life and loved it. She said it was her idea to adopt another dog to keep her company. I wondered if she might be a little disappointed that they chose me but if she was, she didn't show it.

I asked her where we exercised and what time was lights out. She replied that there were no such rules and we could go into the garden whenever we liked and stay up until we were tired.

I asked her if we could eat together and she said as long as I had good table manners, I would be welcome to. That could be a stumbling block. I was used to getting my head deep in the bowl and throwing the food down my neck as fast as I could so no one else nicked it. I always ended up with scraps all over my head and stuck in my teeth.

I vowed to up my game on the eating front and would use a napkin from now on. I really didn't want Dolly to disapprove of anything I did.

She showed me to my digs. My bed was next to hers. Hers was a large, round queen-size with a luxurious deep plush grey pile. I touched it with my paw, which instantly sank to the bottom of the bed. I quickly pulled my paw back out in case I'd left any dirt behind.

My bed didn't disappoint either. Next to hers, it was obviously smaller but just as fluffy. I jumped in and buried my head deep into the pile, then rolled around and around until I was dizzy.

I'm ashamed to say I did leave some skid marks in my frenzy but I brushed the pile over and hoped Dolly hadn't noticed.

CHAPTER 11

The Next Chapter

The first thing my new owners did was give me a bath. Maybe Dolly had mentioned the unfortunate marks on the bed after all.

I'd never had a bath before and I didn't care for it at all. A quick rinse around the key areas would have been perfectly adequate. I really didn't need to have a long soak.

I don't understand humans' obsession with cleanliness. It seems really pointless to me. Why shower every day and then get dirty and then shower again the next day? Just stay dirty. It irritates the hell out of me when I've taken the time to carefully roll in fresh fox poo, making sure I've covered all my crevices in the odour, then I get home and have it all washed off again. I don't want to smell of lavender or bergamot, I want to smell of fox.

My new owners decided I should be called Edward, or Ted for short. I could live with that.

Anyway, I wasn't bothered what they called me as long as I could stay with them and Dolly. I needed a base for my operations. I needed to get my bearings and get that briefcase back, I didn't want to be moved on or banged up again.

After we'd got settled, I asked Dolly if she had a briefcase as I wanted to tell her all about mine but she said she was more into handbags and hers were all safely stored in her dressing room. To see if we had any other common ground, I asked her if she had much experience with explosives but she lowered her head and quietly said, 'You shouldn't play with fire, Edward.'

She was like the mother I'd never had and I adored her right from the start.

She showed me around the garden and I couldn't believe my eyes. There was a fence at the back but nothing at all around the front. I asked her if this meant we could just leave when we wanted to and she looked at me blankly and said, 'But why would you want to?'

She had a point.

Then again she'd clearly not hung out with a terrier before.

Dolly very soon got used to my evening sorties. I told her I would always come back even though I might be gone a while. I know she used to stay up worrying about where I was and couldn't really sleep properly until she'd heard me sneaking back in. I'd tell her I'd be fine but she was the worrying sort.

In the end she gave me a curfew of 2am and I would make sure I was back by then otherwise I knew she'd be cross, fit me with a tracker or, even worse, ground me.

To my utter joy, there was a wood about a ten-minute trot from the house and there were no roads to cross to get there. At first I wasn't sure if it was 'my' woods or not and for several months I searched in vain for any sign of my old hideout.

I discovered the endless joy of badger and fox holes in these woods. It was so dangerous and so much fun. I would force my body into the small holes they'd made by squiggling and squirming until I could get quite far down. I was a lot thinner in those days. If I tried it now I'd certainly get stuck.

I'd push my face in as far as I could until I came nose to nose with the furious occupant. Then I'd flash my teeth and quickly reverse out as fast as I could so I wouldn't get bitten on the face.

The adrenalin coursed through my veins as I made my escape. I imagined this was what it would be like in the SAS, facing danger head on and not flinching in front of the enemy.

As winter arrived and the nights drew in, I spent more time at home and less time in the woods. I'm not a big fan of the cold. I don't really have the coat for it. My coat is great in the rain as water just runs off my back like a duck but it's not very well insulated, just rather greasy.

There was an extensive collection of books in the house so I decided to browse through a few, looking for ideas of what to do with the rest of my life.

There were a lot of autobiographies so I started with those. I'd heard of the comedian Michael McIntyre – I laughed at one of his jokes once – so I pulled his book out first. It was called *Life & Laughing*. The first three pages are all about the colour he selected to paint his home office before he started writing the book. Brinjal no 222 if you're interested. I wasn't so I put it back.

Next I tried Chris Evans' book *Call The Midlife*. I think Chris is a part-time guru and local radio DJ, not that I'd heard of him.

The first chapter in his book started with a top ten list of buckets. (No, me neither.) These included a builder's bucket, a galvanised mop bucket and an ice bucket. I really didn't need to read any more.

Skipping quickly past *Barking up The Right Tree: The Science and Practice of Positive Dog Training* by Dr Ian Dunbar, next on the bookcase was *Mortimer and Whitehouse: Gone Fishing*. The pair on the cover looked like a couple of right muppets but it did seem like they were having fun. The front said 'Life, Death and the Thrill of the Catch', which sounded right up my Strasse.

Of course I knew nothing about fishing but I did like chasing and catching stuff. I knew it was an outdoor pursuit and often ended up in the pub. What was not to like?

CHAPTER 12

My Big Break

Sometime later, over breakfast one morning I overheard a conversation in the kitchen about possibly getting a dog to join the team on *Gone Fishing*. My ears pricked up immediately. I knew this was my big chance. I asked Dolly if she wanted to go for it but she said it really wasn't her thing. She didn't like getting her paws muddy and wasn't all that keen on water either. She said she'd like to appear on *Countryfile* or *Antiques Roadshow* but the chance had never presented itself thus far.

I wasn't going to let this opportunity pass me by.

Later that night I apprehended a phone and, after a bit of trial and error, I recorded a video message and sent it to Bob.

'Hello, Mr Mortimer. My name is Edward and I like pocket meat and explosives. I am trained to SAS rank Warrant Officer Class 1, the highest position possible.' (I wasn't but I'd seen Billy Billingham on *SAS: Who Dares Wins*, who was.) 'I can be your close protection officer on the riverbanks and waterways. I don't take crap from anyone. I can do a perfect forward roll and can catch fish with these.' I bared my teeth. 'I look forward to hearing from you at your earliest convenience. And by the way, I know where you live.'

The next day, I checked the phone as soon as I had the chance but there was no reply. I was livid. Who did he think he was? This was a chance in a lifetime for both of us and I wasn't about to let it lie.

That night I sent another message.

'Mortimer. It's Edward again. I presume you didn't get my last message so I'll give you one more chance. I can make your ratings soar. I presume you've heard of Toto, Lassie or Scooby-Doo? Well, I'm nothing like any of them but I am pretty unique. Give me a chance. I also know where the taller, thinner one lives.'

I think that did the trick. A couple of days later I heard a strangely familiar voice at the door. I could smell Parma Violets and in wafted Bob. He had a very kind face and was wearing odd shoes that looked more like slippers. One sniff of those was one sniff too many, let me tell you.

He stared at me and I stared back. He smiled. I showed him my teeth. He told me to sit. I resolutely stood. We both looked at each other for a while and there was an awkward silence. I performed a perfect forward roll, letting out a little tommy squeaker as I finished the move. It wasn't planned but it broke the ice and Bob said, 'Yeah, you'll do.'

The deal was sealed.

PART TWO

CHAPTER 13

Research and Development

Over the next couple of weeks, Dolly suggested I revised for my new job by reading the *Gone Fishing* book during the evenings. She said it was important to show I knew at least the basics of fishing, even if it was just how to hold the rod properly or how to spot the difference between a salmon and a trout. She also thought it would give me the measure of Paul and Bob. As usual, she was right.

In the first chapter we read (imaginatively titled 'Mortimer and Whitehouse: Gone Fishing'), Paul and Bob talked about the show and Bob wrote: 'Even though two comedians going fishing is nothing like *Antiques Roadshow*, that's the feeling I get when I watch the series.' I thought that made it sound a little dull, if I'm honest, but Dolly said I had to get my favourite TV show, *SAS: Are You Tough Enough?*, out of my mind, that *Gone Fishing* was a far more gentle show with no explosives, which I thought was a shame.

Then we looked at Chapter 7, which was entitled 'How to Fish'. We thought this would be essential reading given my key role on this show.

Paul had written: 'Once you've settled quietly and are nestled in a wooded little thicket by the riverside, hiding from the fish's excellent vision, then you try to think like the fish. Study the terrain ... you are locked into a battle of wits and wills with your quarry. Start to get inside the fish's head.'

This was getting more like it.

Bob had written about the different methods of catching he'd heard about when he was younger. I had to read the next line several times as he said one rumour was that you could throw a stick of dynamite in the water. I read on, panting quite hard by now.

Bob wrote: 'Funnily enough this one is true because I've seen a thing on YouTube where they were blasting a bridge ... You looked down at the river – BOOM! The blast goes off and slowly all the fish come floating up.'

Mind blown. It sounded like it was a battlefield out there, man pitted against beast, deep in the countryside, with the bonus of live dynamite thrown into the mix.

The clincher was in Chapter 13: 'Mortimer & Whitehouse: Gone to the Pub', where Bob wrote: 'Riverbank to Pub, it's an unbeatable combo ... it gets to about four or five o'clock which is a great time for fishing but by that time we're both just thinking of beer and pie.'

I do love a pub. Not one of those fancy gastro pubs that are popping up everywhere these days, I'm talking about a real spit and sawdust proper pub with no carpets and plenty to lick up off the floor. I am partial to a discarded crisp or two. Cheese and onion is my preference.

I was by now beside myself with excitement about joining them on this adventure. Hanging out with two minor celebrities, exploring the flora and fauna, scoping out the local wildlife, stalking the fish and finishing off in a pub. I'd hit the jackpot.

The only thing that put a bit of a downer on my growing excitement was a letter I received a week before my first official engagement.

It was from Pierre. The good news was that he had been re-homed with Lotta, which he described as 'formidable'. The bad news was that Vinnie had finally absconded from the home and was now on the run. He had my briefcase with him. Pierre described this as a 'catastrophe'. I whispered 'fils de salope' under my breath.

Vinnie could be anywhere by now. I knew he had safe houses all over the country and a network of contacts in the underworld.

I clung on to the faint hope that Paul and Bob may be able to help. I'm not suggesting they have any gangland contacts but maybe they knew the team behind

Crimewatch – or *The One Show*, at a pinch. We could do a live appeal on that maybe?

Now wasn't the time to dwell on this. I had to pack and I wasn't about to screw up my one shot at the big time.

The night before I left for the first shoot, Dolly was as reassuring as always. She said I could call her any time of the day or night and she'd always be here, waiting for my safe return. I hoped she wouldn't be lonely without me but she said she'd be perfectly happy doing her nails and bingeing on a box set and I wasn't to worry.

So I started packing my bag. Hairbrush, towel, bedding. I popped in my tuxedo in case there was a formal dinner planned to welcome me to the team. I cleaned my teeth very thoroughly and slicked back my eyebrows. I was camera ready.

CHAPTER 14

On My Way

I was picked up in a silver people carrier the next morning. There was a blanket laid out on the seat and a magazine for me to read. It was *Angler's World* and I can't say it was a page turner.

The drive was about two hours. I amused myself by playing count the lamppost – it's a classic in the canine world, you know how we all love a lamppost. I got to 1,756, which was a personal best. This was a positive start.

When we finally got to the hotel, I was looking forward to meeting everyone. I don't think they were expecting me and I nearly got flattened by various bits of technical equipment and clumsy feet in large boots.

I heard people saying how cute I was so I realised I needed to take control of the situation and make them understand ASAP how tough I was and how I would take no crap from any of them. Start as you mean to go on, Edward, I thought. I took a strong stance in the middle of the room and firmly stood my ground.

I was introduced to everyone aside from the big boss Lisa, there was: John the fishing guide, Rob the director, Stephanie the producer, Louise the production manager, Andre the assistant producer, cameraman brothers Toby and Barnaby, sound man Sam, drone man Andy and two assistant camera operators, Matt and Nat.

They were a rather motley bunch, all in all. I could immediately understand why they needed someone like me to bring some glamour and style to the team.

I was taking it all in and sniffing each individual thoroughly when I was summoned to another room to have a private meeting with Paul and Bob. My little paws started to sweat and I think I let off another tommy squeaker but I held my head high and sashayed into the room. After all, I was to be their security detail.

Bob immediately put me at ease with a piece of pocket meat. It was a little stale and it had lots of fluff stuck to it, but I ate it anyway. Paul shook my paw warmly and as he released it, I muttered, 'And away.' Bob overheard and they both smiled.

Paul welcomed me to the team and briefly laid out the rules: Mind the rod, do not bark at the fish, don't get under Bob's feet and under no circumstances wind the reel.

I think the last one was a reminder for Bob.

I then laid out my rules for them: No touching unless I expressly give permission, do not expect me to come the

instant you call me, fresh pocket meat to be available on demand and a nightly pillow treat.

They looked at each other, shrugged and nodded their agreement to my terms.

After we'd set out our parameters, there was an awkward silence in the air. I took the opportunity to lick some dirt out of my ears while I waited for them to speak again.

I'm not very good at small talk. It's always seemed pointless to me but I do understand it is deemed to be polite. I don't know if picking your ears in public is polite but needs must.

Eventually, I said, 'Do either of you know why dogs always sniff each other's butts?'

They both looked blankly at me so I decided to drop the proverbial canine bombshell and reveal the truth.

One day, many, many years ago, all the dogs in the world went to a massive house party. It was one of the earliest canine raves. A little bit like my birthday parties, it was legendary.

All breeds, shapes, colours, sizes, anyone who was anyone was at this party. It was the place to be on four legs.

As everyone arrived, the cloak dog, a rottweiler called Dave, took everyone's tails and hung them up on several tiered racks, giving each dog a numbered ticket in exchange for their tail.

The party was in full swing, everyone was on the dance floor, drinks were flowing, the music was pumping, sweet dog treats were being surreptitiously passed around ... then suddenly, the fire alarm went off.

Smoke started to billow into the room. You couldn't see your paw in front of your face.

There was utter panic. All the dogs rushed at once to the exits and simply grabbed the first tail they could get their claws on.

In the ensuing carnage, hardly anyone ended up with their own tail.

Miraculously no one was killed but now every dog has a duty to sniff each tail they encounter, to check if it might be their original tail.

As I finished my superb story (which by the way is entirely true), the silence in the room was deafening. Paul and Bob looked at me for a second. Then they both looked at my tail (or where my tail should have been), then they looked back at me.

'Mine didn't make it out,' I said quietly as my nubbin rocked from side to side.

Bob lifted up his shirt and showed me the scar where he'd had his heart operation a few years before. It was certainly a whopper. 'We all have battle scars, Edward,' he said.

I wondered if Bob had previously been in the SAS. I thought he probably had and that this might come in very handy later down the line.

Paul then said, 'Enough of this nonsense. We need an early night as we are off as soon as the sun's up in the morning.' I could immediately tell Paul was the boss of this partnership and the brains of the whole operation.

Before they could haul themselves out of their chairs, I was out of the room like a rat up a drainpipe. It was going to be my first night in a hotel room and I was ready for it.

My room was small but warm and comfortable. I did have a treat left on my pillow, which I thought was a nice touch. I ordered a light supper of steak frites and forced myself to have a quick shower so I'd be a little fresher in the morning. I didn't fancy sleeping on the bed. How do you know who else has slept in it? So I settled down on the bath mat.

CHAPTER 15

Faffing and Fishing

The next morning I experienced a level of faffing I have never seen the like of.

I wake up. Yawn. Stretch. Go out. That's it. Ready for action in under one minute.

Not this lot. Not a bit of it.

There is faffing about coffee, clothes, shoes, boots, waders, sugar, snacks, tea, rods, bait, nets, notebooks, phones, more faffing about coffee, sunglasses, ground sheets, easy-ups, hats, socks, batteries, microphones, cameras, coats, rucksacks, drones, radios, chargers, camping stoves, ingredients, bags, loading and unloading and loading again and a final extra coffee faff.

Then they were ready to leave.

But then someone forgot something, so back we all went. And then someone wanted another coffee. I felt like going back to bed. These people needed a firm paw for sure.

To clarify, that is 'leaving' faff – there is then 'arrival' faff when we get where we are going, which is pretty much exactly the same routine in reverse.

I got to travel in Bob's car. He wouldn't let me sit up front as that's Paul's rightful place, but I didn't mind as there was so much to explore in the back.

Bob's car is extraordinary. It's like being in an amusement arcade. There are bits of food everywhere, ground into the seats and on the floor. There are packets of sweets and sugar wherever you sniff. On that first trip I found half a Scotch egg, a chicken wing and some Frazzles. I loved it.

We got to the fishing spot and, after a lot of aforementioned arrival faff, Bob and Paul settled into their camping seats to fish. I scoped out the area for any potential threats and to secure the wider perimeter. Once I felt we were all safe, I wandered back to them and looked for my seat. They must have left it in the car, which I was pretty miffed about. I decided to settle down between them both, but not before I trod on Paul's rod to make my feelings clear re the lack of chair.

They were fishing for pike. An adult pike has 300–700 teeth (puts my 42 to shame), which are as sharp as razors, and I can't say I was looking forward to coming face to face with one.

As Paul and Bob quietly fished, I took some time to make a few mental notes about them.

Bob reminds me of a fly. He loves sugar and he secretes it everywhere he can. He's also quite sticky, which is why I enjoy licking him.

He has such a sweet tooth. In fact, he has quite magnificent teeth, not as sharp as mine but much whiter. He once said it would be great if he could have my bottom teeth and I could have his top teeth, which would certainly work for me. My top teeth are a shambles.

His pockets are never empty and there's always such a wide variety of sugary goodness in them. I did wonder if the weight of those snacks is what affects his balance. He spends a great deal of time on the floor. Perhaps he just wants to get closer to me or see the world from my point of view.

He's not bad at fishing, but I prefer it when he sits chatting with me on the bankside. So does Paul.

I told Bob all about my briefcase and how Vinnie had escaped with it. He was incredibly sympathetic and said he'd help me look for it in any way he could. He told me he'd lost a holdall once and it still bugs him to this day.

He said we'd make every effort to track down this Vinnie chap and that he couldn't have got very far on his stubby little legs (he meant Vinnie's legs, I'm pretty sure).

I plucked up the courage to ask Bob if he had a military background. He smiled enigmatically and whispered, 'Night manoeuvres.' I told him I also enjoy midnight sorties and we chatted about our different adventures.

I'm afraid I can't tell you much more as it is highly classified information.

Paul is an excellent angler. His eyes lock on to the river as he fishes. It reminded me of when I was surveying my squirrels in the woods. It's like the world around you stops and your entire focus is on the task at hand. He looks majestic and clearly loves the entire experience. It's wonderful to watch him in full flow, carefully casting time and again to target the fish.

He gets cross when Bob disturbs him with annoying questions like 'What's your favourite jam?' or 'What's the best oven temperature?' It really makes me grin, especially as I often feed Bob the questions.

Paul thinks I am capable of bringing down a sheep. In truth I could probably take on an entire fleet of sheep if I wanted to. I might look slow but I can really accelerate when needs be. I have never harmed a living being in my life, it's just not my style. I know I look like a killer but that's just a front. Anyway, sheep aren't really that much fun to play with. I do work out, mostly press-ups and pull-ups to try and maintain my shape. I'm fully aware I'm fighting a losing battle. I put on weight easily – it's the eating between meals that does for me, so I do need to watch it. I've never really had any willpower with food though. It just tastes so damn good.

Time really slows down on the riverbank. It's a rather magical place. I can see why fishing is so popular. There is space to really stop, think and reflect. Usually I'm far too busy arsing around to devote my time to any of those things. But as I lay there, watching Paul and Bob in the river, I took stock of my life so far. I thought about my mother. Was she still alive? I wondered what my brothers and sisters were doing. I thought about Peggy and John and hoped they were still very happy. I wondered if Pierre and Lotta would start a family soon.

I was abruptly awakened from my daydream by manic shouting. We were under attack. This was what I had trained for. This was why I was there. I just didn't expect front-line action so soon. I sprang up, ready to defend our territory.

There was chaos. People were running around all over the place. Paul was shouting. The cameramen were trying to get to the bankside. Bob had fallen over – I'm not sure if he'd been taken out or had tripped. There was no time to think. I tried to take stock of the situation and remain as calm as possible.

Turns out, Paul had caught a fish. To be fair, it was quite a big pike. I rushed over to see what help he needed, particularly as Bob was still flat on his back.

The pike was now in Paul's net. Boy, was he ugly. The pike, not Paul.

It was quite prehistoric-looking and I gazed at it in awe. I didn't get too close – not that I was scared, I didn't want to get in Paul's way. I was there to assist proceedings, after all.

Bob soon joined me and Paul and all three of us looked at the fish.

Then they put it back in the water. I don't know what I expected but it seemed strange that after hours and hours trying to catch the damn thing, they just put it straight back.

Bob and Paul chanted, 'And away' in unison and off it swam, back to its mates, I imagined with quite a story to tell about being briefly captured by two men and a dog.

Mission had been accomplished and everyone was accounted for. Calm was restored. It was lovely to see the huge smiles on everyone's faces. I was very proud that I'd kept them all safe during their time of need and justified my position on the team.

I rolled around in the leftover fish juice on the riverbank and nicked a bit of bait while everyone was busy congratulating each other. I wondered what would happen next but I didn't have to wait long for the best words of the day: 'Let's go to the pub.'

Bob and I ran back to the car. I am much, much faster than him and easily got there first. To be fair, Bob was still in his waders.

When we were all safely in the car, we cracked open a bag of Jelly Babies to celebrate. I wasn't allowed to eat one but I was allowed to lick the green ones, which no one else wanted.

CHAPTER 16

The Great Bankside Bake Off

Bob is, of course, in charge of the bankside cooking and he takes this responsibility very seriously. So do I. You need to have quite a strong stomach to watch the process unfold close up.

Full disclosure: I cannot cook. My food has always been trapped. There is a good variety of trapped dinners for dogs so I am not complaining. I do prefer fresh chicken or a rare steak but I understand these can be pricey and, with the cost of living business, I'm not about to make unreasonable demands. Not yet.

I'm always offered the leftovers from their bankside cuisine so I watch the little chef very carefully to assess whether I will actually eat it or not when they have finished. Paul doesn't have that choice – he has to eat what is put in front of him and boy, does he put on a brave face sometimes.

Occasionally Paul slips me food from his plate without Bob seeing. If I don't like the look or the taste of it, I scurry

into the bushes and quickly bury it. I thought Bob might notice as I often come back with mud and crap all over my face, but most of the time they are too busy chatting.

Bob's cooking can be a tad dry. Paul has said it's like eating mortar sometimes. It does tend to stick to my teeth but then again, most things do. I can't really blame Bob for that.

He once heated up some military ration packs but none of us could stomach them. It was rank, and for a dog to say that gives you a good idea of the taste of it.

To be fair to Bob, he has rustled up some edible food bankside. My favourites have been:

- Tuna Melanie with Trapped Potatoes
- Park and Ride One Pan Chicken Pilaf
- Not Now Madam Venison, Cabbage and Chestnuts

They do try to be heart healthy, and I'm pleased to report all of the above ticked the right boxes. Tuna, chicken, venison and chestnuts seem to help keep cholesterol at bay.

I'm not going to mention what they often have in the pub when the cameras are not rolling. Pie.

There are superfoods for dogs as well, you know, which might surprise you.

Sweet potato, watermelon and carrots, in particular, are packed with antioxidants and vitamins, which are really good for us.

I don't see the point of sweet potatoes; they should be illegal. Potatoes should not be sweet. Someone's having a laugh with that. Carrots are OK and I cannot eat watermelon. It takes me about a month to get all the pips out of my teeth. It seems a lot of work for a small amount of pleasure. I'll stick with my trapped dinners and the occasional carrot stick, if I really have to.

I help the crew clear up after Bob has cooked, which I know they are very grateful for. There's no dishwasher out in the wilds so I lick the plates and the cutlery until they are really shiny. If you see him, please don't mention this to Paul. He's much more into hygiene than me or Bob.

One of my favourite moments on the riverbank is when we all down tools to have a cup of tea. Bob is a master of the Kelly kettle, firing it up effortlessly in all weathers. It's a powerful bit of kit. It's like having an instant boiling-water tap about your person. I love watching Bob play with fire. It makes my hackles rise, which is technically called piloerection, by the way. It's the canine equivalent of human goosebumps, when the hairs on our back stand up.

When it's time for a break, the lads slip their waders off. I say slip. They tug and pull and huff and puff and moan and groan until they are finally released from their rubbery enclosures and are at ease. Have you ever smelt inside a well-worn pair of waders at the end of a day? Don't. I mentioned before about the amount of smell receptors we dogs have and I can tell you it takes days for the heady mix of feet, sweat and fish to leave my nose.

Paul and Bob can chat about everything and nothing. Their conversations range from cheese to death to paint colours via hair loss. The very best bit is when they make each other giggle. I have no clue what is quite so funny but it makes me laugh just watching them.

It made me realise the importance and true value of friendship. I don't know if I would have survived doing time in the kennels without my pals Peggy and John. Everyone needs someone to talk to and someone to listen to them. And we all need a good laugh every now and then.

It takes your mind off missing briefcases.

CHAPTER 17

A Dog's Life

I gained a unique insight into human behaviour during my fishing trips with Paul and Bob. They showed me a completely different side of people, which I didn't know existed before.

My first experiences with the two-legged variety hadn't been that great and I didn't realise us dogs could be so loved and respected and indeed wanted by you humans.

In my first two homes I was just an irritant, even to my own mother, and in the kennels there was really no time for anyone to show much affection to the inmates, although of course they did care for us and feed us.

I'd heard that dogs were supposed to be a man's best friend, I just hadn't experienced that for myself up till now. Dolly had tried to reassure me that people could be kind but I had found that hard to believe.

Who would get a dog (even if it was only in exchange for a pack of iced mince pies) and then give them to charity like an old jumper or chipped mug? Just don't bother to get it in the first place. Isn't that a simple solution for all of us?

Some of the stories I heard in the kennels would break the hardest of hearts.

I think the worst was from Lulu, who was one of those doodle mixes. Razzledazzleadoodle, I think. Nice looking lady, she was. Anyway, in one night of madness she ended up pregnant (no judgement from me, we've all made mistakes) and when she had the puppies, she was kicked out and left by the side of the road with the puppies in a bag for life. The irony wasn't lost on her.

She reckons she was there for a couple of days before someone spotted her and the kids and took them to the shelter.

The youngsters were quickly fostered because we all know no one can resist a puppy but Lulu beat herself up for being so irresponsible. I know she missed the kids as well but as she was so pretty, she wasn't at the home for long.

Another chap I met in the exercise yard was a retriever type called Eric. He had been kept as a stud dog. When he explained what this meant he had to do on a regular basis, I didn't know whether to laugh or cry.

We certainly were a motley bunch in that place but we all looked out for each other and shared our stories in group therapy sessions, which always began the same way:

'Hi, I'm Eric. I was a stud dog.'

'Hello, I'm Lulu. I was an unfit mother.'

'Hi, I'm Hugo. I ran away from my abusive family.'

Do you know there are currently around 100,000 dogs without homes in the UK? To put this into context, 36,000 people live in Monaco. So even if every single one of the residents of Monaco took a dog each, there'd still be 64,000 wandering about homeless.

Monaco is on my bucket list actually. Must remember to mention filming a Christmas special there to Paul and Bob. Although I gather the quarry there are big game fish like tuna, spearfish and swordfish and let's be honest – they probably couldn't handle those beasts.

If you are thinking of getting a dog, the fundamental rules are very simple, even for you humans to grasp. Feed us, walk us and don't leave us alone for very long. It's not tricky, is it?

It's got to be easier than looking after your partners. We don't give a crap about birthdays or anniversaries, we won't argue about money, and if you get home drunk from the pub, we'll still be very happy to see you. Most importantly, we'll never be unfaithful.

Just remember to pick up our crap, right?

And don't forget, I'll always be watching you …

CHAPTER 18

Friendship

Paul, Bob and I bonded over our similar personal circumstances. None of us have parents in our lives any more. I really liked the way they both spoke so openly about losing their parents and how it shaped their lives. Boy dogs are very like human men – we don't show our feelings and rarely cry or howl. But there's something about being amongst nature in the fresh air that encourages you to share your feelings. I'm not going soft, by the way. I'm still as hard as nails on the inside.

Bob didn't really know his dad as he died when Bob was a kid. I, of course, didn't even know who my father was and I doubt he even knew of my existence. Paul had incredibly happy memories of fishing with his dad, so we all had very different but relatable experiences of our fathers.

They asked me what traits I thought I got from my dad. He was clearly a bit of a ladies' man and I've only had one date so we're not similar in that respect. But I do think my independent spirit and determination came from him. I did sometimes wonder if I got my teeth from him. I like to think I did. I also had an inkling that my briefcase was originally his but I couldn't prove that, not yet anyway.

I enjoyed listening to their stories about their own kids. I'm not sure I'd have the patience to have little pups running rings round me. Although I'd be strict, I'm not sure I could be arsed with the constant clearing up. Anyway, I'd not met anyone I could spend the rest of my life with, apart from Dolly, and that would be a whole bowl of wrong.

It was easy to forget the cameras were there. Paul, Bob and I just did our own thing – they fished and I farted about – paying no real attention to the crew all around us.

It took a while for me to let my guard down properly with the camera crew. I didn't want all my private business broadcast to the world so I was a little cautious of them to start with.

I was also in awe of them. They stand for hours on end in rivers and lakes getting the shots they need. They hardly move a muscle. You've probably seen me paddling out to them – I'm just checking in with them to see if they're OK. I can only last about five minutes in the rivers as it's so cold but they never complain. At least, not to me.

I've heard that they pee in their waders. I'm not judging. I know it keeps them warmer in the water. But here's an odd thing: I can't go in the water. I can go by the water or near the water but I can't cock my leg *in* the water. I just fall over.

Crew lunch is always fun. Everyone sits around on camping chairs, scoffing sandwiches and biscuits for about an hour. I have totally nailed my begging face. Eyes as wide as they can go and a little drip of drool falling from my mouth into their laps. I can hold this stance for as long as necessary to get a titbit. The most important thing is never to avert the gaze. I also try to make myself look really thin by sucking in my stomach so they feel sorry for me. That move is getting harder to pull off by the day, to be honest.

What really annoys me though is the sauces humans put on perfectly good bits of meat. I hate mustard – just have the ham. I hate mayonnaise – just have the beef. And don't get me started on pickle. What the hell even is that? Why ruin a cheese roll with what looks like lumps of dog dirt in gravy?

After lunch some of the crew have a little forty winks so I take the opportunity to have a wander and explore the surrounding area. It's just an extra patrol I like to do, FOC.

You may have wondered why I often wear a loud bell on my collar. It's because they know I like to wander off and it helps them locate me. What they don't realise is that I slip my collar off as soon as I am out of sight so I can have total freedom to do whatever I like. I need my privacy sometimes, which I'm sure you understand.

My PB for going AWOL is three hours. I had planned on just the two hours but managed to get myself a little lost. I was listening to Notorious B.I.G. and just lost track of time as well as the actual dirt track I'd taken.

When I sauntered back, I could tell people had been worried, which was a really nice feeling. Someone actually cared about where I was. I wanted to promise not to go missing for so long next time but I didn't want to make a promise I couldn't keep.

A word in your ear now about our collars.

Do NOT put our names on our tags. I can just about live with the fact we have to always have ID about our person but don't put our names on them. Think about it. If we're nicked, people will know what to call us. Just make sure we are microchipped. It doesn't hurt and keeps us safe. Got it?

Talking of names, after you have given us one, for crying out loud, use it. Pack in the nickname nonsense. It's a downright epidemic amongst you owners. I'm surprised we ever remember the original name you gave us.

Oh, one other thing. Please do NOT clip the poo bag dispensers onto our leads or harnesses. Carry them yourselves, you lazy buggers.

Lecture over.

CHAPTER 19

Sleeping Arrangements

Once the fishing is finished for the day, it's time for my favourite part of the show – the overnight accommodation. Paul genuinely doesn't know where he'll be staying and neither do I. Bob keeps it a secret from both of us. He's smart and devious like that, most probably because of his SAS training.

I get really excited as we approach where we're staying. My nubbin goes into overdrive and I jump up on the back shelf of Bob's car so I can get the best view. I usually go in first, mainly because Bob and Paul are getting on a bit now and can take ages to get out of the car, moaning about their stiff backs or heavy legs, so I take my chance to cross the threshold first. I have to stop and pee on the gate or fence or bushes, obviously, just to leave my mark, then I head on inside.

I scope the place out, checking the general security arrangements, and then have a good sniff around the kitchen area. This has a dual purpose: looking for vermin and/or any crumbs. Once I've given it the all clear, I head upstairs.

I recce the bedrooms first. I jump up on the beds and roll around, counting the pillows, assessing the general comfort rating and checking the tog level of the duvet.

Then I wait to see which bedroom they pick and I'll sleep with whoever has, in my opinion, chosen the best room. I do feel a little guilty about the one who misses out on sharing with me. They sometimes seem a little disappointed but they hide it well.

For clarity, I should mention I don't sleep *with* either of them. I now have my own pop-up bed, which travels with me. I know a lot of dogs like to sleep with their owners on the bed but my relationship with Paul and Bob is on a more professional level and I don't want to blur any boundaries.

They say you shouldn't mix business with pleasure. *Gone Fishing* is a pleasurable business but still, a line needs to be drawn.

Besides, I find the thought of sleeping in a human's bed rather unsavoury, whoever they are.

I'm not the best roommate, to be honest. After a long day outside, I like to lick my paws for approximately four hours, then I like to clean out my ears with one paw, which means I need to lick that paw again for another couple of hours. It is a relatively noisy process but it has to be done.

Have you ever wondered why dogs sleep so much in the daytime? It's because they are usually up half the night. I thought it was just me who suffered from insomnia but when I was in the kennels the noisiest time by far was during the middle of the night. I asked around and hardly any dog there had a full eight hours' sleep. They usually just grabbed a couple of hours here and there.

Dogs are neither diurnal (meaning they are active in the day and sleep at night) or nocturnal. Bet you didn't know that. Well, now you do. And do you know what else – we keep an eye on you ALL night.

Paul and Bob sleep relatively well. There are a few nocturnal movements and emissions but nothing I wouldn't expect from two mature men after a busy day out in the elements.

I would, of course, continue to watch over them both until my alarm went off for breakfast.

Some of the places Bob picks do not allow dogs to stay and this does not sit well with me, considering what an integral part of the show I am. It's not like I demand my own room. I'm happy to share and I always wipe my paws, if not always my butt.

The first time there was no room at the inn, as it were, I packed my bag and thought I'd settle down in the nearest woods to sleep. I was disappointed but I don't mind the occasional night outside. It keeps my senses sharp and my training up to date. It would also be a good opportunity to check for any signs of Vinnie or my briefcase.

I was about to disappear into the night when one of the crew said I was welcome to go with them. They were staying in a nearby pub, which was more than happy to take dogs. This was an exciting turn of events. I didn't say goodbye to Bob or Paul, to make my feelings crystal clear, just jumped into the waiting truck with gusto.

CHAPTER 20

Party On

The crew van was a totally different travelling experience. It was jam-packed with technical crap and I had to squeeze myself in beside some cables and gaffer tape. It was not quite the comfort or style I was used to but I didn't care as they cranked up the party tunes on the stereo and off we whizzed, singing along to the Vengaboys. It was like we'd all been let off our leashes after a hard day's work. There was a real party atmosphere and I decided this should continue.

When we got back to the pub, with the big bosses safely tucked up in their accommodation, I suggested we threw a little crew party. They'd all heard about my legendary birthday bash at the kennels and were pumped for it, so I told them to leave all the organising and finer details to me.

We ordered takeaway from a well-known fast-food chain, which I'm pleased to report tasted very much like dog meat, but the crew didn't seem to mind that.

Then we got busy on the karaoke machine. I've never sung karaoke before but I took to it like a duck to water. I thought I sounded magnificent as I belted out 'Kung Fu

Fighting' by Carl Douglas with some signature karate moves thrown in.

The crew's faces were a sight to behold. Their eyes were as open as their mouths. Some even covered their ears.

We finished the night on the floor singing The Gap Band's 'Oops Up Side Your Head'. I thought it was so kind of them to choose a song and dance I could join in with, although I have no clue what it was all about.

They said they didn't usually party like this while Paul and Bob were out of sight, but I'm not sure I entirely believed that.

It was a long, late and mildly debauched night and I enjoyed every minute, especially the bits I could actually remember.

The next morning I was very bleary-eyed and it didn't go unnoticed. I heard Bob say to Paul that he thought I'd been crying all night as I wasn't allowed to stay with them. Bob took me to one side and apologised and said that whilst it was sometimes out of his control, wherever possible from now on, he'd make sure the accommodation would accept dogs. To be honest, I wasn't bothered because if it meant I got to stay with the young gang again, bring it on, I thought. They were party animals, that lot, and I have the utmost respect for each and every one of them.

They did find work tough going the next day and I felt a bit sorry for them. I slept most of the time and got away with it as Bob and Paul just thought I was still sulking.

CHAPTER 21

Special Guests

We don't invite many other people to join us on *Gone Fishing*. I say 'we' as Paul and Bob always consult me on who they are thinking about inviting. I check them out with Dolly, who knows more about showbiz stuff as she reads *Grazia*, so is up to date with who is in and who isn't. I prefer *Soldier*, which is the official magazine of the British Army.

I've made some great new friends doing this show and learnt so much more than just the rudiments of fishing.

I learnt to play the guitar so I could perform on stage with Paul Heaton and Jacqui Abbott in Newcastle. We did an exclusive rendition of 'Caravan of Love'. It was a pinch-me moment.

It was the most nervous I've ever been on the show. I'd been practising with that guitar for weeks. It's not easy to play with my fat little paws but I went at it with gusto and determination. I wasn't going to miss this chance to impress our Paul, who also plays guitar, and yes, I admit, to also advance my showbiz career.

Paul and Jacqui were so accommodating, you'd never know they hadn't ever played with a Patterdale before. Their voices are like silk together. I did join in on one chorus but my harmonies were a little off so they suggested I stuck to the guitar solo.

We smashed it.

People were saying afterwards that I should head-line Glastonbury. I've seen some of the coverage of that carnage and whereas the amount of mud is sublime, I can't do crowds that size. I'm used to an outside toilet but even I draw the line at the state of those Portaloos.

I learnt an important lesson about my anatomy when Richard Herring joined us for supper after we'd fished a tributary of the Thames.

I think I threw him a little as I turned up in my full tuxedo. As I recall, he said it was like sitting next to George Clooney. I don't know who he is but I presume he's incredibly good-looking and suave.

Richard was there to talk about his book *Can I Have My Ball Back?*, which is all about his journey to recovery from testicular cancer. He explained that he had to have one testicle removed and now instead of two he only has one. He talked about how important it was for men to check for any unusual lumps or bumps 'down there', as he put it.

I jumped down from the table and immediately went to my room to check my balls. I couldn't see or feel any trace of them. Had I lost them or had they fallen off somewhere? Did I pack them in my briefcase? I didn't remember. There was certainly no sign of them about my person. It was very unsettling. Where the hell had they gone?

I didn't want to worry Paul or Bob as I knew they were working (I use that term loosely) so I waited until Richard had finished his dinner (again I use that term loosely, as Bob cooked it), left the table and was on his way home. I followed him down the drive and pawed at him until he bent down to greet me and then I came straight out with it.

'I can't find my balls, Richard. Am I going to die?'

He said, 'Ted, mate, you've probably been neutered. You won't have any balls.'

I was stunned. Who did this to me without my consent?

Richard gently picked me up, which I wasn't keen on but given he was in a similar boat on the testicle front, I allowed it on this occasion.

He explained to me about how many dogs, particularly strays, which I suppose *technically* I was, are neutered for health and safety reasons. That it was a common and highly recommended procedure.

I wondered why they hadn't left me with the one, like Richard, but I guess it was too late now and what was gone was gone. I thanked Richard for his candour, and we went our separate ways.

I didn't re-join Paul and Bob later that night. I had to come to terms with what I'd learnt, not least realising I could never have kids even if I wanted to. I went straight to bed and yes, I did have nightmares.

I promised this book would tell all about what happens behind the scenes on *Gone Fishing*. The following is probably one of the more personal and sensitive things I've had to write.

When Bob was laid up with The Shingles (I gather that's a virus, not a band), the lovely comedian Lee Mack joined me and Paul on the stunning Burgh Island in South Devon. It's the most incredibly romantic place and that week it was gorgeously warm and sunny, with not a cloud in the sky. The whole scene was idyllic.

While Paul fished off the rocks for wrasse, Lee and I spent a lot of quality time together. We strolled around the island looking over the cliff edges at the nesting sea birds, flew a kite, picked shells off the beach, paddled in the sea and had afternoon tea together before taking time out to meditate and then doze side by side in the sun. I laughed at all his jokes and he gently stroked my back and rubbed my ears.

Yes, we had a bit of a holiday bromance going on.

Paul and Bob were none the wiser about this and Lee and I agreed that what happened on Burgh Island stays on Burgh Island, so I can say no more about it.

I have to be respectful as Lee has his own pet dog back at home and I have no wish to break up a happy family.

Talking about memorable friends of the series, I have to blow Charlie Cooper's trumpet. He joined us on the River Severn and brought with him an extraordinary homemade sausage roll in the shape of a fish, which he didn't hesitate to share with me, even though Paul and Bob told him I was watching my weight. I actually wasn't. They were watching it for me. Anyway, it was one of the tastiest things I've eaten bankside and he even gave me the leftovers to take back to the hotel that night. Legend.

One of our most regular guests is Dr Anand Patel. He's so smart. Paul and Bob seem to have an endless list of various ailments, complaints, aches and pains to question him about but nothing foxes Anand. I think he likes hanging out with us and he's always talking about how getting out and about in the countryside is so good for you, especially if you are feeling a bit low. It made me realise why some of the dogs in the kennels were a bit depressed. Dogs shouldn't be kept in cages, they should be allowed to roam and run free.

Unless they were a felon called Vinnie with a stolen briefcase.

CHAPTER 22

Explosive

There is one standout moment from my time on *Gone Fishing*, something I will never forget. It was quite literally BANGING.

It was a Christmas present from Paul and Bob and it was a dream come true.

When we were filming the Hogmanay special up in Scotland, we'd invited Clare Grogan and her band Altered Images to play. They were famous way before my time as I gather they were big in the eighties, so obviously Paul and Bob, being the age they are, knew their music really well. I didn't but it didn't matter – they were really chuffed to meet me and I enjoyed hanging out with them. I also had a real soft spot for Clare and I don't think I was the only one.

While the band were playing, the production team had arranged for a huge firework display to light up the night sky. I know a lot of animals don't like fireworks and I get that – they're incredibly loud and the bangs seem to go on forever. Dolly hated them. They made her violently shake, so when it was that time of the year, she was given some doggy Valium in her dinner. I accidentally ended up eating it once and was really spaced out for hours, which was a right laugh.

It probably won't surprise you that I LOVE fireworks. I love the bangs, the noise and the smell of explosives hanging in the air long after the display has finished.

Paul and Bob said I should stay inside while they were being let off and I was gutted.

I told them I wouldn't be scared but they said it was for health and safety reasons. Bloody red tape.

But then they surprised me. They said, 'How would you like to actually set off all the fireworks?'

I couldn't believe my ears. Me? And a detonator? With my paws ... and my reputation?

I was led into a small, dark side room and there, standing majestically before me, was a huge red button on a long wooden plinth. Paul said when they gave the signal, I was to push the button with both my paws as hard as I could to ignite the fireworks.

I can tell you now I had a full-on piloerection. My hackles were right up.

When the moment came, my mouth went dry. I took a big deep breath, then pushed with all my might and – BANG – I heard the fireworks start outside. I rushed to the window to have a look at my handiwork. It was a truly magnificent display.

It took some time for my paws to stop shaking. The adrenalin was coursing through my veins for what felt like hours afterwards. Happy New Year indeed!

CHAPTER 23

Who Do I Think I Am?

One of the most common questions I get asked is: 'What happened to your teeth?' Closely followed by: 'What breed are you?' I find both questions a little impertinent. I don't greet any human I meet by asking who their parents are or demanding to see their birth certificate.

I vaguely remembered what my mother looked like but of course I never knew my father, so I decided to take a DNA test. I have put a copy of the certificate on the next page, but these are the headlines:

I am a mix of Belgian Malinois, Rhodesian Ridgeback and Bulldog.

Let that sink in. My first thought was for my poor mother. She was quite a slight thing, as I recall, and those are big boys.

I was 40–60 per cent Malinois, 10–25 per cent Ridgeback and Bulldog.

I like the fact I have Ridgeback in me. They were bred to bring down lions so that does explain my speed and agility. But I'm mostly Malinois so let's take a quick look at their traits, according to the American Kennel Club:

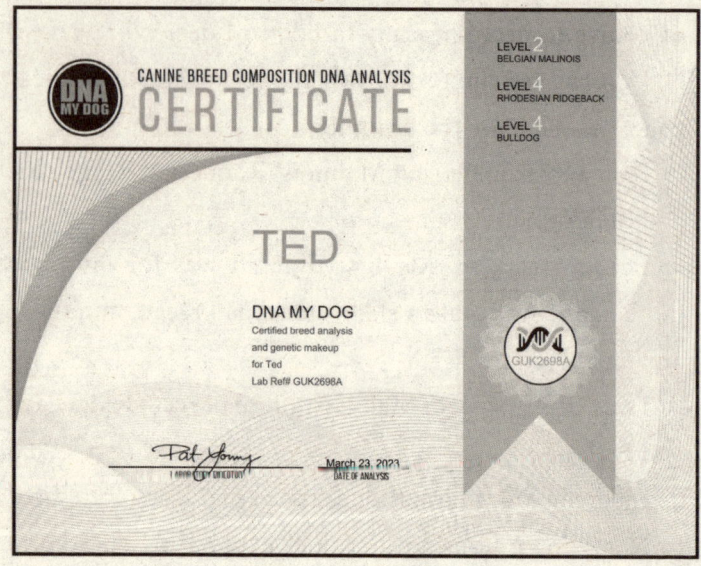

CANINE BREED COMPOSITION DNA ANALYSIS
CERTIFICATE

LEVEL 2
BELGIAN MALINOIS

LEVEL 4
RHODESIAN RIDGEBACK

LEVEL 4
BULLDOG

TED

DNA MY DOG

Certified breed analysis
and genetic makeup
for Ted
Lab Ref# GUK2698A

March 23, 2023
DATE OF ANALYSIS

GUK2698A

'The smart, confident, and versatile Belgian Malinois is a world-class worker who forges an unbreakable bond with his human partner. Mals are squarely built, proud, and alert herders standing 22 to 26 inches. Strong and well-muscled, but more elegant than bulky, there's an honest, no-frills look about them, as befit dogs built to work hard for their feed.'

I'll take world-class, proud, strong and more elegant than bulky, thank you. I don't like the fact they shortened Malinois to 'Mal'. That's like calling me a Pat.

I'm not sure what to say about the Bulldog part. Their description is as follows:

'The Bulldog is a thick-set, low-slung, well-muscled bruiser whose "sourmug" face is the universal symbol of courage and tenacity.'

I'd been called various things but 'sourmug' was a step too far in my book.

There was apparently not a trace of terrier or indeed Patterdale within my DNA.

As far as I'm concerned, if it looks like a Patterdale, walks like a Patterdale and hunts like a Patterdale, I'm a Patterdale.

(Ted Tip – don't spend your hard-earned money on dog DNA tests.)

CHAPTER 24

Love Is Not in the Air

My love life. This will be a short chapter.

I've had one date, which Paul and Bob set up for me. I was so excited and packed my special floral shirt to wear, but when I went to put it on, I realised I'd also put on a few extra unwanted pounds and I kind of bulged out of it. The buttons were really straining. Paul reckoned I'd look better without it and although that left me feeling a little exposed, I think he was right. Besides, I might have taken someone's eye out if a button flew off.

They both gave me a pep talk about what to talk about and how to behave. I was really nervous and nearly backed out of the whole thing. I didn't really need a bitch in my life. I had my BFF Dolly at home and I didn't fancy being under the paw of another woman.

But as they'd set it up, I felt I had to go along with the date. It's really not easy doing this kind of thing on camera either. I watched a few episodes of *First Dates* and *The Undateables* to get some tips but it just made me more nervous. My teeth were chattering as I got to the riverbank

where we were meeting. And with my teeth, it sounded like a chainsaw had started up.

I knew she was a Patterdale called Effie. Paul and Bob had shown me a picture. She was younger than me but not in an inappropriate way. She was very pretty, with brown eyes and dark fur. She was athletic too. She clearly worked out.

I checked my teeth and licked my whiskers. I practised my opening lines. 'Hello, I'm Edward.' Paul said I wasn't to mention my explosives hobby, so I went with, 'Do you favour a briefcase, handbag or clutch?'

The boys sent me off to meet her. She took one sniff of me and ran in the opposite direction. And she could run really fast. There was not even a backwards glance.

That's the last time I nick Bob's aftershave. I don't think it mixed well with the smell of fish and pocket meat.

So that was my one and only date, over before it really began. I'm not ready to get back into the dating game any time soon. I'd rather hang out with my mates.

Paul and Bob felt bad for me, I know they did. Paul even let me tread on his rod without shouting at me and Bob gave me a solid portion of pocket meat.

I'm now a confirmed bachelor and happy to stay that way. Bitches can be tricky.

CHAPTER 25

Dress to Impress

I have a walk-in closet at home. It's a bit like a cardboard box and I can open the side flaps and browse through my latest outfits. I'm not into designer labels. My fashion style is more akin to Bob's – practical and, above all, cheap.

I loved dressing up as Santa Claus, I felt very special wearing my birthday hat and bandana and I thought the tuxedo was stand-out, but my favourite outfit is probably the security guard jumper, which did unnerve Paul a bit. It's the one outfit I also wear at weekends, even though I'm officially off duty.

I particularly like to dress up for our annual awards ceremony, as do Paul and Bob. It's one of the highlights of our *Gone Fishing* year. Although I will admit I do usually sleep through most of it. Like all awards ceremonies, it does tend to drag on a bit.

We're all keen to win the top trophy, Employee of the Year. It's such an important accolade and a real recognition of the graft we've not really put in all year.

No one knows the results, as they are in sealed envelopes, and there's a real tension in the air before Bob announces the winner.

Quite rightly, I have won twice now, while Bob and Paul have won once each. I think theirs was a sympathy vote.

The thing about awards is that they don't really matter, unless you win, of course.

The programme editor, Mr Doug, cuts my speech out of the episode though. He says there is no time to include it, which I'm not sure I believe. So for a special treat, here is what I prepared to say which has never been aired before:

'I have a dream where other dogs will one day live in a nation where they will not be judged by the state of their fur or by their backgrounds but by the content of their character, that all dogs will be created equal.'

Well, I was hardly likely to thank my mother and father, was I?

Recognition is good but I didn't intend to become famous. I will admit it has given me a certain swagger. I'd love to know if any of my brothers and sisters have seen me on the TV. They've not been in touch, of course. I wonder what they'd say to the shrimp of the litter if they could see me now. Not so much of a runt, eh?

Fame hasn't changed me at all. I think when you have humble beginnings you fully appreciate it when life takes an unexpected turn for the better.

I don't intend to cash in on my popularity. I felt this book was important to get my voice heard and set the record straight, but there will not be a sequel anytime soon. I might actually turn my paw to fiction and write 'The Cold Case of the Missing Briefcase'.

I have been thinking of launching my own dog cologne, as I can see a gap in the market for that. I'd call it Totally Ted, or Essential Edward for the premium range. It would have hints of fox, blackberries and leather with subtle notes of sulphur. It would be a scent both humans and dogs could wear with pride, with the tag line 'Be happy, smell sweet'. I'd split the proceeds between my first care home and the fund to find my missing briefcase.

But a word of caution here – fame won't guarantee your happiness.

CHAPTER 26

Life's Too Short

It's been wonderful being the star of *Gone Fishing* and I wouldn't change a thing about any part of it.

I consider myself really lucky to have been given this opportunity, especially as I know I'm not a particularly good-looking chap and I have my faults. And odd teeth.

If I could change one thing, it would be the life expectancy of dogs. It's just too short and it's simply not fair. We don't get a good crack of the whip. Just as we get settled and life is sweet, we are staring down the barrel of a gun. The bigger the dog, the smaller their life expectancy.

I'm twelve in dog years, which is 70 in human terms, so I'm considered to be a senior citizen of the canine world. That also makes me slightly older than Paul and Bob but I, like them, have no intention of slowing down or retiring. Not while there is still fish in our rivers, meat in their pockets or a briefcase at large.

I reckon I've got a good five years in me yet but even that just doesn't feel long enough.

Bob and Paul talk about their own mortality a lot on the series and that has really helped me come to terms with the fact there is a finite time we are on this earth, and we need to live in the day as much as possible, being grateful for the small things and appreciating our friends and family. I think this becomes more important as you age as time really does seem to speed up the older you get, and the years just fly by. Particularly for us dogs, as we only get one year for your seven – which is both discriminatory and pretty harsh to accept.

When it's your time to go, Paul and Bob would say, make sure you don't regret anything and are at peace with the world.

One thing I've spent quite a bit of time thinking about is that none of us have the choice of dictating when it's our time to go. The ideal for both humans and dogs is to slip away quietly in our own beds but sadly that is not often the case.

Humans can take the incredibly difficult decision to end their dog's life if it is suffering. I often think how hard that must be for you but what is equally wonderful is we get to leave this world, safe in your arms, knowing how very loved we are. That is such a precious gift you humans can give us and, on behalf of all the dogs you've ever loved and lost, thank you. It's the kindest thing you can do for us.

When my time comes, I expect to have a funeral with full military honours and to be cremated in a coffin made of steak. I would like Paul and Bob to do a joint eulogy and for my highlights from *Gone Fishing* to be played on a loop throughout the ceremony.

CHAPTER 27

The End

I was glad we'd spoken so openly about the end of life because I got home from one particular fishing trip quite late and Dolly was fast asleep in her bed. I crept in beside her and gave her a hug as I always did when I returned from a business trip.

She immediately woke up and I noticed how peaky she looked. She said she was feeling tired and her joints were aching. I asked her if she'd had a particularly busy day and she said she'd just been in bed all day.

I looked into her eyes. They were a beautiful sea-blue colour but had misted over a few months ago. Her hearing was a little dodgy now as well, so I leant into her ear and whispered, 'You'll feel better tomorrow and we'll go for a light brunch in the café by the woods and I'll tell you all about my trip.'

She nuzzled into me and I noticed her breathing was quite heavy. She must have been really tired. I felt a little guilty about going away on one of my jollies when she had clearly needed me to be around.

She quietly said, 'Edward, I want you to know you have changed my life for the better. I am ashamed to say I used to look down on rescue dogs, I thought there must be a reason why no one wanted them, that in some way they were a lesser dog than a pedigree. You've made me realise that quite the opposite is true. Having a second chance at life makes them so grateful and joyful to be around. You truly deserve to be a star. Now go clean those teeth!'

I told her to stop being so soft, even though she was spot on.

She told me she hoped I'd find my briefcase one day and that I could always use one of her handbags in an emergency. I didn't have the heart to tell her I couldn't risk ruining my macho image. I thanked her for her kindness as always.

I think Dolly knew it was her time. She was almost 14, which is a good, if not necessarily fair, age for an Old English Sheepdog.

I realised she was old but I suppose I always thought she'd go on forever. She was the one person I truly loved with all my heart and I couldn't bear the thought of life without her by my side. She'd always been there for me, never judged me even when I was at my naughtiest and loved me unconditionally.

I said, 'Sleep well. See you tomorrow.'

It was only when I got back to my bed that I couldn't stop the tears from falling. I prayed to Lassie and promised I'd never nick another piece of pocket meat if I could spend just one more week with Dolly.

In the morning Dolly's bed was empty. Her favourite toy, a little woolly sheep, was now in my bed. I knew she'd gone. The whole atmosphere in the house had changed. Grief swamped me and I could hardly breathe. I ran out of the house and continued running. I didn't know where I was going and I didn't care. I was trying to outrun my feelings of utter despair.

Eventually, exhausted, I stopped. I was in the bluebell woods where Dolly and I had often walked and played. There was a carpet of bluebells in full bloom, and it was a really beautiful, tranquil scene. I lay amongst the flowers for an hour or two, reliving my fondest memories of my best friend. I was so grateful to have had her in my life, however short it now seemed.

When I got back to the house, I picked up the *Gone Fishing* book. In the final chapter, appropriately titled 'The End', Bob had written:

'It's terribly sad when old fishermen part, isn't it? You see two old blokes, fishing in their sixties or seventies – at some point they're going to lose their buddy.'

I had lost my buddy.

But I'd gained two very special friends in Paul and Bob and I will always be grateful for that.

There are friends, there is family, and then there are friends that become family. As M.K. Clinton said, 'The world would be a nicer place if everyone had the ability to love as unconditionally as a dog'.

Postscript

At the time of going to print, Vinnie is still at large and my briefcase is still missing.

Please can I ask each and every one of you to keep an eye out for it. On the left there is a drawing of what it looked like. I imagine it will be dirty and dishevelled by now but I would love to have it back.

If you see it, please message me on my Instagram: @ted_gonefishing

There is a reward for its safe return. But it has to be my exact briefcase with the correct six-number combination to unlock it.

Appendix

Will

Ted would like to leave his bed to veterinary medical science; what they'll find ground into the fabric could provide an important breakthrough in the future health of all dogs.

Ten Golden Rules
for Dog Ownership

1. Never shout at us – talk to us, we understand more than you realise.

2. Please don't take your phone out on a walk; take in the surroundings, we know when you are not paying us attention and it's as much your walk as ours.

3. Let us roll in anything we fancy. It may not suit your tastes, but we love it and we know you're going to clean us up later anyway, so we'll take the hit for a good, dirty roll.

4. Let us come to the pub with you. It won't cost you anything and we love being around humans, especially when they drop crisps and snacks on the floor.

5. We know when you are sad, so whisper your troubles into our ears – we'll listen for as long as you want to talk.

6. Let us sniff. We need to sniff as much as you need to break wind. Both are natural habits and a form of personal expression.

7. Listen when we bark – we're usually trying to tell you something is wrong.

8. Take the time to train us properly – there's plenty of classes around. I feel so bad for the dogs who only get walked on leads or spend too much time home alone.

We can get just as lonely and bored as you – remember we always have each other.

9. Please vary our meals – would you fancy dry crackers every day for breakfast, lunch and dinner?

10. Don't prolong our suffering. Look into our eyes – we'll tell you when it's time. Remember, you can never be a day too early but you can be a day too late to let us go.

11. When we've gone, please don't forget us – we'll always be waiting for you.

12. We can't count.

Ted's Treats

When I was at my naughtiest, although I would say at my most adventurous, there was one thing which would instantly lure me out of the woods. Here is the recipe. I suggest you enlist the help of a grown-up when making this.

1 packet of liver – pig or chicken
2 eggs
A dash of milk
Garlic if you fancy (my breath is bad enough without this addition)
150g wholemeal flour

1. Shove it in a blender, mix it all up. It looks and smells rank at this stage, although I do enjoy licking the spoon.
2. Line a baking dish with foil and pour the sticky goodness in.
3. Bake at 180°C for around 40 mins.
4. Leave to cool and then cut into little squares.

Tip: I store mine in the freezer and take some out for each walk

Last Known Contents of Briefcase

- Compass
- Squirrel charts and data – various sizes
- Blanket – threadbare and stained
- Mirror – 2cm square, with pearl handle
- Cocktail sausage and cheese leftovers (possibly mouldy)
- Used chewing gum (mint)
- One and a half firelighters
- Copy of *The Satsuma Complex*
- Spare tooth
- My missing testicles x 2 (unconfirmed)

How to Train a Patterdale

What I Have Learnt about Fishing Techniques

Unacceptable Pocket Meats

Secrets I Know about Bob and Paul

What did you expect, they're secret.

References

Muppets

You've no doubt heard me refer to Paul and Bob as a pair of 'muppets' … in case you wondered which characters I specifically meant:

Statler (Bob) and Waldorf (Paul).

The resemblance is uncanny, isn't it?

Briefcase

Finally, if you are in any doubt about just how important briefcases are, this is the way they are described on the internet:

Briefcases are serious and fall in the 'classic' formal category.

As they're often manufactured with leather, you will usually find them in sober black and brown colours. Formal briefcases suit the senior professional and adults. Someone who has been through the highs and lows of professional life.*

I rest my (brief) case.

Edward 2024

---

* Hasan, M., 'The Backpack vs Briefcase Debate', *Alaskan Leather Company* (2021), https://alaskanleathercompany.com/blog/backpack-vs-briefcase

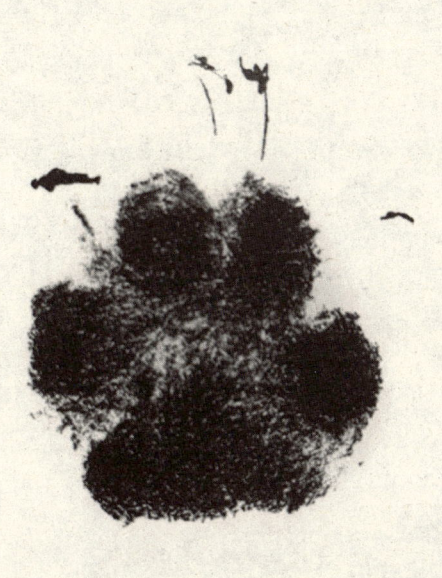

Acknowledgements

Ted would like to thank:

Bob and Paul for being two of the most wonderful muppets to hang out with.

The whole *Gone Fishing* gang: Stephanie, Louise, Andre, Georgia, Rob, John, Toby, Barnaby, Andy (aka Adam), Sam, Matt and Nat, not forgetting Doug, who always makes me look magnificent in the edit.

The Diana Brimblecombe Animal Rescue Centre, who took me in and still work tirelessly to help so many unwanted and abandoned animals.

Karina for always looking after me when I can't go fishing.

Becki for keeping Bo off my back and teaching her some manners.

Lisa would like to thank:

Bob and Paul for being two of the most wonderful humans to work with.

Caroline Chignell and Claire Nightingale at PBJ Management, Jacquie Drewe and Gordon Wise at Curtis Brown.

Lorna Russell, Michelle Warner, Marta Catalano and Shelise Robertson at Ebury.

Jamie Munro and Camilla Cope at Greenbird.

Catherine Catton and David Brindley.

Dan, for making sense of it all.

Jon-Joe and Archie for making me so very proud every single day.

Finally, Dolly, Ted and Bo for their unconditional love and loyalty.

Read on for an exclusive sneak peek
at Ted's next book, Pup Fiction, *coming autumn 2025…*

Prologue

I've had my briefcase for as long as I can remember. It was always very special to me. I think it's because it was all I ever really owned in the world. I'd been in four different homes before I was seven months old and it became like a security blanket for me.

Then I left it behind in the woods and someone else took it. It's remained my primary mission to get it back and who'd have thought that undertaking would lead me to foreign climes and a daring rescue mission, worthy of any blockbusting film.

Many people have asked me what's in the briefcase and why getting it back means so much to me.

Maybe the answer lies with the film supremo Quentin Tarantino, who said the value of the briefcase in his classic 1994 movie *Pulp Fiction* lay not in its contents but in the briefcase itself.

You could draw that analogy with fishing as well. It's not always about the fish you catch and just as much about the joy of fishing itself. Being on the riverbank with

Paul and Bob is one of the greatest pleasures in my life, alongside food and most recently my passion for parkour.

All these delights are about to collide in one big European adventure and you are most welcome to join me on the ride.

Do you know what they call a quarter pounder with cheese in France?

Turns out, I was about to find out.

The Life of an Author

My first book, *A Pawtobiography*, was published in November 2024 and rocked the book world off its very axis.

I don't want to wag my own tail, but the fact is I outsold many of my heroes, like Al Pacino, Cher and David Jason.

And I shifted more copies than Rick Astley.

The whole journey, from being an unwanted skinny runt to a star of the small screen and then a best-selling dog author, was a hoot.

Sure, I get recognised these days. I don't really mind but it can be quite awkward when I'm in the middle of a major clear-out in the park of a morning. It's not the ideal time for a selfie or a pawtograph. Let's just say the most eager fans get a little more than they bargained for when they bend down to greet me – a right noseful, in fact.

Has it changed me? You can judge for yourself in this book.

Spoiler alert: No.

I did get quite a bunch of fan mail, with plenty of offers to boot.

Aslan wrote to me from the dental practice where he works in Turkey, offering me some new veneers.

Edgar wrote from a clinic in Latvia offering me free weight-loss injections.

I declined both, not because I was insulted by their offers, far from it, but because I wouldn't have the first clue how to get there. Otherwise I would have been bang up for a bit of a makeover.

I know I have 'unusual' looks but that's what makes me stand out from the crowd. I only get miffed when people openly laugh or point at me and ask if I'm related to Rylan. His teeth are not natural, I'll leave it there.

I will admit to being slightly miffed that with all those millions of readers, no one managed to find my bloody briefcase. Did you even bother to look?

Honestly, if you want a job doing properly, you have to do it yourself, as you'll find out.

I'm getting on a bit now and I should be able to spend more time relaxing in bed. To be honest, I do spend 80% of my time asleep but the other 25% it's all go go go.

I made it clear in my last book, maths is not my strong point and it has not improved.

So, here we are at the start of another canine-flavoured adventure.

What can you expect from this book? Well, I ain't saying. You gotta pick it up and plough through it yourself. You made your bed, go lie in it. Lucky sods.

About the Authors

Ted has co-starred in BBC2's *Mortimer & Whitehouse: Gone Fishing* since Series 3 and is now an integral part of the popular show, keeping Bob and Paul on their toes. He is mostly Patterdale Terrier – although a DNA test revealed some surprising results. He is 12 years old and lives in Surrey but travels a lot with his fishing work. This is his first book.

Ted's trusted co-author Lisa Clark has been producing entertainment and comedy shows for over 30 years – from *The Big Breakfast* and *Don't Forget Your Toothbrush*, to *Shooting Stars*, Vic & Bob's *House of Fools* and *Mortimer & Whitehouse: Gone Fishing* since it began in 2018. Lisa lives with Ted, a Briard called Bo, her current husband Dan, and occasionally her sons, Jon-Joe and Archie.